The Writer's Table.

The Writer's Table.

FAMOUS AUTHORS AND THEIR FAVOURITE RECIPES

Valerie Stivers

ILLUSTRATIONS BY
KATIE TOMLINSON

Contents

Introduction: Eat Your Words

To eat or drink together is a fresh encounter with a favourite novelist

Inspired by a scene in a story by Russian novelist Nikolai Gogol wherein the devil whizzes dumplings into a character's mouth, in 2017 I began a long-running project for *The Paris Review* of cooking food from the pages of classic novels. I'd choose a dish that seemed to represent the spirit of the work and then research or make up a recipe for it, chopping and slicing and frying and baking my way through books like Herman Melville's *Moby-Dick* or Virginia Woolf's *To the Lighthouse*. During the process I discovered a strange affinity between what felt like the writer's spirit and how the food turned out. D.H. Lawrence, who watched the industrialization of his native English countryside with horror, wrote about living close to nature and pursuing a simple, good life centred on physical love. The dinner I made from his work was delicious and deeply nourishing. A despairing writer, like Intizar Hussain, who wrote about the tragedy of partition in India and Pakistan, produced a meal where everything went wrong – a Pyrex exploded; I cut myself; the *jalebis* didn't turn out.

In some cases, the dinner surprised me and even carried a message that gave me new insight into the book. Kafka's food was awfully good for someone with a nervous stomach who wrote a story about a man waking up one morning from uneasy dreams to discover he'd turned into an *ungeheueren Ungeziefer* (horrible vermin, depending on your translation). The caraway-seed-encrusted crunchy pretzels (page 99) that I made from his novel *The Castle*, and the four-ingredient apple cake from *The Metamorphosis*, turned out so well that they reinforced a mystic Kafka interpretation of my own: Kafka's darkness is bursting with hidden light, and all his winged creatures are angels. You can tell because the food is good.

In the book you hold in your hands, I have culled recipes not from great writers' work but from their lives, as well as provided biographical sketches on their eating habits. This material is illuminating in a different sense. Discovering what a person eats can tell us quite a bit about who they are. Roald Dahl, creator of *Charlie and the Chocolate Factory*, loved sweets as much as the kids in his stories do, and kept a jar of wine gums next to his bed for midnight snacking. From this we suspect that he never quite grew up – and that it's the secret to his books' taboo-breaking, off-kilter appeal. In his writing, Dahl punishes the guilty spitefully and with sadistic glee: crushed by a giant peach or drowned in a river of chocolate. But he gets away with it because the punishments feel safely cordoned off in childlike innocence and fantasy.

The literary food stories collected herein are as varied as the writers themselves. Maya Angelou gained confidence from her cooking; Joan Didion made domestic perfection one more notch on her belt; Colette liked to eat the same way she liked sex, and she had no shame about either. The stories are arranged alphabetically, and the earliest occurs in 1547 with Miguel de Cervantes, and then travel the globe, with an unavoidable focus on works written in English from America and the UK. The youngest writer included is Han Kang, born in 1970, a Korean woman who was the winner of the 2024 Nobel Prize in Literature. There are twice as many authors again whom I could have included and didn't, purely for considerations of space.

Many great writers have said throughout the years that their biographical details are irrelevant to the enjoyment of their work. For the writer, nothing matters but *the book,* the soul externalized. The reader understands this, however, which is precisely why we *do* want to know them. Love the book, love the man. It's only an enhancement of our pleasure as readers to know that D.H. Lawrence devoted his life to the kind of passionate monogamous love he wrote about, and that he's voluble and often irritable when the food is bad. Sensuality mattered to Lawrence. And it's wonderful to see Barbara Pym, writer of a series of witty British dating comedies, dining alone in order to observe others eating, and taking notes all the while. The love she wrote about in her books eluded her, but she took greater joy in writing anyway.

In many cases it was possible to pair the writer with a recipe, either one they wrote or used, or one that scholars or other authors associated with them. A few, like the recipes of mine reprinted from *The Paris Review*, have been made up in homage. All are presented in the spirit of historical documentation, with original measurements (or lack thereof), terminology that has not been standardized, vintage cooking instructions or implements, and no promise of success or failure. The only ones I've tried are the ones I've written myself. But succeed or fail, to make any one of them will be a great story.

– *Valerie Stivers*

Maya Angelou
1928–2014

Friends drop by

Caramel Cake

Serves 8

• 8 tablespoons (1 stick) butter • 1¼ cups sugar • ¼ cup Caramel Syrup (recipe follows) • 2 cups sifted all-purpose flour • 2 teaspoons baking powder • ½ teaspoon salt • 1 cup milk • 2 large eggs • Caramel Frosting (recipe follows)

Preheat oven to 375°F. Line two 8-inch layer cake pans with greased wax paper.

In large mixing bowl, beat butter, and add 1 cup sugar gradually until light and fluffy. Beat in syrup.

In medium mixing bowl, sift flour, baking powder, and salt together. Add sifted ingredients to creamed mixture, alternating with milk.

In separate medium mixing bowl, beat eggs about 3 minutes, until foamy. Add remaining sugar, and beat until there is a fine spongy foam. Stir into cake batter until blended.

Divide batter between cake pans. Bake for about 25 minutes. Remove pans from oven. Gently press centre of cake with forefinger. Cake should spring back when finger is removed. If it doesn't, return to oven for 10 minutes. Cool in pans for 10 minutes. Turn out onto rack, and remove wax paper. Let cakes cool to room temperature before frosting.

To assemble: Centre one cooled cake layer on cake plate. Cover top and sides with generous helping of frosting. Place second layer evenly on frosted layer. Repeat frosting procedure. Make certain that sides are completely frosted. Cool in refrigerator until ready to serve.

Caramel Syrup

• 1 cup white sugar • 1 cup boiling water

Heat sugar in heavy skillet over low heat. Stir constantly until melted to a brown liquid. When it bubbles over entire surface, remove from heat. Slowly add boiling water, stirring constantly. Pour into container and cool.

Caramel Frosting

• 6 tablespoons (¾ stick) butter • One 8-ounce package confectioners' sugar
• 4 tablespoons heavy cream • 1½ teaspoons vanilla extract • Pinch of salt

Brown butter in heavy pot over medium heat – be vigilant or it will burn. Allow butter to cool. In large mixing bowl, add confectioners' sugar, cream, vanilla extract, and salt to the butter, and beat until smooth. If frosting is too stiff, add tablespoon of half-and-half or full cream to thin.

– From *Hallelujah! The Welcome Table: A Lifetime of Memories with Recipes* by Maya Angelou

Maya Angelou's hospitality was legendary, and after she became famous with the publication of her 1969 autobiography *I Know Why the Caged Bird Sings*, she made friends with other legends, and cooked for all of them. The writer James Baldwin once accepted an invitation to an Angelou picnic that ended up lasting for thirty hours. Angelou made a traditional French cassoulet for food writer M.F.K. Fisher; smothered chicken for Oprah Winfrey; and a feast of crowder peas and okra and baron of beef (a top sirloin roast) for a crowd of 150 for a meal in honour of Toni Morrison celebrating her Nobel Prize. She hosted an annual Thanksgiving celebration at her home in Winston-Salem, North Carolina, and an annual New Year's Day feast of traditional foods like black-eyed peas and roast chicken for her friends in New York. 'If Maya Angelou likes you, even just a little bit, she wants to cook for you,' the *LA Times* once proclaimed.

But Angelou wasn't always confident in the kitchen. When she was seventeen years old and a single mother of an infant son, living in San Francisco and desperate for money, she took a job in the kitchen at a restaurant called The Creole Cafe. The only dish she knew how to make was rice, though she could do that perfectly – 'till each grain stood separately', she writes in *Hallelujah! The Welcome Table*, the first of her two cookbooks. The restaurant was offering seventy-five dollars a week, too much to pass up, so Angelou asked the cook at her mother's boarding house what 'Creole food' was and got her knives out. (His advice: onions, celery, red peppers, garlic and tomatoes, 'put that in everything'.) Despite her tender age and lack of knowledge, she set the restaurant's menu herself, and quickly found herself 'embroiled in the mysteries of the kitchen with the expectancy of an alchemist about to discover the secret properties of gold'.

Little wonder she was good at it. Cooking, for Angelou, was a form of communication, whether with the 'light-skinned French Creoles from Louisiana' clientele at the restaurant, or with her famous guests, family and friends. 'Indeed, I feel cooking is a natural extension to my autobiography,' she told *The Guardian* newspaper in 2011. And her appetite for autobiography was nearly as great as her appetite for food – she wrote seven of them. She also saw no stigma in writing about food. She added: 'I know some people might think it odd – unworthy even – for me to have written a cookbook, but I make no apologies.'

Angelou learned about good food from her grandmother, Annie Henderson, or 'Momma', who took in Maya (born Marguerite Annie Johnson) and her brother Bailey when their mother couldn't keep them when Maya was three years old. Henderson was born in slavery and cooked over a wood stove for most of her life, Angelou told the *LA Times* in 2004. She'd learned to cook using the undesirable foods – livers, lungs, gizzards, feet – given to slaves. 'With almost nothing, if you care, you can make something. That's the lesson of African American cuisine.'

'If Maya Angelou likes you, even just a little bit, she wants to cook for you' the *LA Times* once proclaimed.

Hallelujah! The Welcome Table shines in its early sections when Angelou relates Henderson's recipes. She tells about the crackling corn bread that she looked forward to after the smelly and difficult work of processing every bit of the whole hog, which Momma insisted she watch. There's also an 'unimaginably good' lemon meringue pie, the star of one of Momma's favourite jokes. But the most poignant recipe in the collection is the caramel cake that was Momma's show-stopping contribution at quilting bees (a gathering for people to communally complete quilts). Angelou was mute for five years after being sexually assaulted at age seven – the event that was the subject of *I Know Why the Caged Bird Sings*. One year, a new teacher publicly humiliated her and then slapped her for not being able to talk. When Momma found out, she marched over to the school and slapped the teacher back. And then she made Angelou the caramel cake, showing that Momma too knew how to use food to communicate her love.

Jane Austen

1775–1817

Pleasing her own appetite

White Soup

Make your gravy of any kind of Meat, add to it the yolks of four Eggs boiled hard & pounded very fine, 2oz of sweet Almond pounded, as much Cream as will make of it a good Color.

– From *Martha Lloyd's Household Book: The Original Manuscript from Jane Austen's Kitchen*

Jane Austen was interested in food, wrote about it often in her novels and, surprisingly, given the drawing-room comedies she is beloved for, grew up connected to the land. At Steventon Rectory where Jane was born, Austen's clergyman father George had a glebe farm (one provided as part of his church living), and also rented land nearby, which he farmed for profit. The family kept a cow for fresh milk and butter, and 'were used to good fresh food', according to Sophie Reynolds, director of the Jane Austen's House Museum in Hampshire, England. After her father's death, Jane lived with her mother and sisters at Chawton Cottage, where the museum is now located. The Austen women had orchards and vegetable gardens, picked the fruit from their own apricot trees and grew currants. Their brother Edward, lord of the nearby manor, supplied them with milk, butter and cheese from his dairy.

Austen didn't cook herself, but the houses she lived in were small, and she would have been in and out of the kitchen and 'seen everything taking place', Reynolds says. At Chawton, the household labour was divided such that the nearly-seventy-year-old Mrs Austen did the gardening, sister

Cassandra did most of the housekeeping, and Jane was responsible only for breakfast. Most of her day was devoted to writing, and it was while living at Chawton that she succeeded in having her first three novels published, and composed her last three.

In the Austen family's later years, family friend Martha Lloyd lived with them in Southampton and at Chawton, and did most of the cooking. Lloyd kept a household book, a hand-written manuscript with recipes including those for home remedies ('A certain cure for a swell'd Neck') and things like making ink. The volume has become an invaluable source of insight into Austen's daily life; when Austen mentions a specific dish in her letters or in her work, in some cases there's a recipe. *Martha Lloyd's Household Book* was finally published in 2021, around 200 years after it was written, with annotations by Austen scholar Julienne Gehrer. In addition to the recipe above, the book has the pea soup from an Austen letter, when she mentions that she'd dined on 'pease soup, a spare rib and a pudding'. The recipe calls for peas (presumably dried), celery, onions, anchovies, mint, parsley and spinach. Lloyd also has a recipe for a pudding, made with bread, suet and apples ('boil it three hours in a Cup').

Though the historical record is scant when it comes to Austen's life – only 161 letters survive of the thousands she must have written – we have every reason to think that Austen was a passionate person who enjoyed her life, good company and drink, Reynolds says. At one point, when she's been left in charge of the family meal-planning, she tells Cassandra with her trademark acerbic wit: 'My mother desires me to tell you that I am a very good housekeeper, which I have no reluctance in doing, because I really think it is my peculiar excellence, and for this reason – I always take care to provide such things as please my own appetite, which I consider as the chief merit in housekeeping. I have had some ragout veal, and I mean to have some haricot mutton tomorrow.'

Reynolds notes that period-piece recreations of Austen's novels, though set in the Regency era, tend to mistakenly suggest an aura of Victorian delicacy and refinement. Austen was a Georgian: a member of an earthy society where people were not ashamed of their bodies and plumpness was a virtue. The Prince Regent (from whom the Regency takes its name) led the way in enjoyments of the table, and there's every reason to think that Austen followed suit. On one occasion she even admits in a letter that her hands are shaking as she tries to write, because she drank too much the night before. Reynolds believes that we can also suspect a particular interest in matters of the table because Austen describes the details of foods eaten by the characters in her novels, in comparison, say, to details of dress, which she does not much describe.

Austen's genius for biting social commentary shows nowhere better than in the food references in her novels. It's used to display social status, as when Mrs Bennet in *Pride and Prejudice* is determined to have 'two courses' when she has Mr Bingley over for dinner – she means this not in the modern sense of a starter and a main meal, but as two sequential full spreads on an extravagant table groaning with food. Often, and more humorously, people's eating habits display their neuroses, as when, Mr Woodhouse, a kind man but overly concerned about his health, tries in *Emma* to prevent the guests from eating his daughter's wedding cake, or suggests to all and sundry that they try a nice bowl of thin gruel as an after-dinner digestive – an offer with few takers.

The most famous dish in the Austen oeuvre, however, appears in the following lines from *Pride and Prejudice*. Mr Bingley declares the Netherfield Ball 'a settled thing,' and adds 'as soon as Nicholls has made white soup enough I shall send round my cards'. The white soup recipe from Martha Lloyd's book, reproduced above, hardly sounds like a showstopper for a ball, but the dish has its roots in Medieval English and French court cooking, and is sometimes called by the more elegant names, *potage blanc* or *soup à la Reine*. Austen may have intended the dish to be a joke, both bland and pretentious; to joke about food was very like her.

Honoré de Balzac

1799–1850

The founder of food in fiction

The famous *rilettes* and *rillons* (a kind of sausage meat) of Tours formed the larger part of our midday luncheon, between breakfast in the morning and late dinner at the hour of our return home. This preparation, highly prized by some epicures, is rarely seen at Tours on any genteel table; though I may have heard of it before going to school, I have never been so happy as to see the brown confection spread on a slice of bread for my own eating . . . My school-fellows, almost all of the shopkeeper class, would come to display their excellent *rilettes*, and ask me if I knew how they were made, where they were sold, and why I had none.

– From *The Lily of the Valley* by Honoré de Balzac

Honoré de Balzac had a huge belly, round face, bulbous nose and a reputation for extremes – his masterwork, *La Comédie Humaine*, includes ninety-one finished works and runs to thirty-four volumes in some editions. He also enjoyed feasting to grotesque excess, and was rumoured to drink fifty cups of coffee a day. Nonetheless, his precise attention to detail and complex characters made him a founder of literary realism and an influence on great realists to follow, such as Flaubert, Dickens and Henry James.

Balzac fell in love with literature during his early years, as an escape from a life of privation and emotional hunger. He was unhappy first in his bourgeoise family home, ruled by his harsh, ambitious father and a mother disinterested even by the standards of the time. Then, at age eight, he was sent to a boarding school whose contract specified that students could not return home during the entire period of their schooling, and whose meagre dining-hall fare was expected to be supplemented by contributions from the student's family. Balzac lived at school for six years, was visited by his parents only twice, and received no supplemental food. Anka Muhlstein, the author of *Balzac's Omelette: A Delicious Tour of French Food and Culture with Honoré de Balzac*, writes that his schoolboy hero Félix de Vandenesse in the novel *The Lily of the Valley*, quoted above, expresses the writer's longing for the tasty food his schoolmates received, and his shame at having none.

Whenever Balzac was finished with a piece of work or had sold a book, however, he indulged in orgies of food.

Hunger of a more abstract kind – for satisfaction in life – followed Balzac into his adulthood, when early attempts to enter the legal profession made him despair. He wrote in an 1821 letter to his sister that he did not want to be 'a clerk, a machine, a riding-school hack, eating and drinking and sleeping at fixed hours. I should be like everyone else. And that's what they call living, that life at the grindstone, doing the same thing over and over again . . . I am hungry and nothing is offered to appease my appetite.'

The young Balzac loved to read, and often did so at school when he was being punished with time in solitary confinement. Writing, which he embarked upon in the 1820s, satisfied his cravings for a meaningful life, but it did little to help him eat better. The writer kept to a draconian regime, always arising at 12a.m., 'chained to his desk from midnight till dawn', having a light meal at 5 or 6p.m., and then going to sleep, according to *Balzac: A Biography* by Graham Robb. '"I have taken an axe and severed all ties,"' Robb quotes him as saying during a period of productivity. He wrote very rapidly with a quill and produced huge word counts. During periods of intense activity he barely ate at all, 'in order to avoid wearying the brain with digestion', he explained, according to a quotation furnished by Muhlstein. His early death at fifty-one (gruesomely, of gangrene associated with congestive heart failure) was attributed to his over-consumption of the coffee he used as fuel for his feats of writing.

Whenever Balzac was finished with a piece of work or had sold a book, however, he indulged in orgies of food. During one episode mentioned in Muhlstein's book, he ate 'a hundred oysters as a starter, washing them down with four bottles of white wine, then ordered the rest of the meal: twelve salt meadow lamb cutlets with no sauce, a duckling with turnips, a brace of roast partridge, a Normandy sole, not to mention extravagances like dessert and special fruit such as Comice pears'. Graham Robb recounts strange feasts, such as one in which he served his guests only onions (onion soup, onion purée, onion juice, onion fritters . . .) and says he could gorge himself 'like a camel at an oasis'. During the fruit course, Robb writes, Balzac would 'remove his cravat, undo his shirt and demolish a giant pyramid of pears or peaches, homing in on "those twisted, desiccated fruits with black patches . . . under whose skins Nature enjoys placing exquisite tastes and odours"'. The biographer notes this as a 'cheering contrast' to the privation the author felt staring at his schoolmates' *rilettes*.

Italo Calvino

1923–85

The baron in the trees

Tree-nut Tart

Serves 12

• 120g (4¼oz/½ cup) butter • 100g (3½oz/½ cup packed) dark brown sugar • 80g (2¾oz/¼ cup) golden syrup (light corn syrup) • 2 tbsp granulated sugar • 120g (4¼oz/1 cup) toasted, salted cashews • 100g (3½oz/⅔ cup) toasted, salted, Brazil nuts, chopped • 65g (2¼oz/½ cup) blanched whole almonds • 40g (1½oz/⅓ cup) salted, shelled pistachios • 30g (2oz/¼ cup) toasted pecans • 2 tbsp double (heavy) cream • A 23cm (9in) pre-baked shop-bought or homemade pastry case (tart shell) • ½ tsp coarse salt

Preheat the oven to 180°C/350°F/gas 4.

Make the filling. In a small saucepan, combine the butter, brown sugar, golden syrup and granulated sugar. Cook over a low heat, stirring until the sugars dissolve. Increase the heat, and whisk until the mixture comes to a boil. Continue boiling until large bubbles form – about 1 minute. Remove the pan from the heat, add the nuts and cream, and stir.

Place the pastry case on a baking sheet, pour in the nut mixture, and spread out evenly. Bake for 20 minutes, or until the filling bubbles. Leave to cool to room temperature and serve.

– Adapted from a recipe by Valerie Stivers for *The Paris Review*

The first chapter of Italo Calvino's 1957 novel, *The Baron in the Trees,* is entirely devoted to the description of a family meal, in which the young hero, Cosimo Piovasco di Rondò, pushes away his unwanted dinner – a gruesome plate of snails – and runs away from the table to climb a tree, where he will stay for the rest of his life. Cosimo is fleeing the kitchen-work of his mad sister, Battista, whom Calvino describes as being 'a skilled cook, because she had both diligence and imagination, the prime talents of every cook', but who devoted her talents to making the most disgusting possible meals. The family confronts crostini with a pâté of mouse liver, cake set with a mosaic of locusts' legs, pig tails roasted like ring cakes and a porcupine cooked whole with all its spines. Fancy-work includes heads of cauliflower adorned with rabbit ears, a pig's head with a lobster emerging from its mouth, and creme puffs with snails' heads stuck on them.

Calvino was a writer of big ideas who liked to play structural games in his fiction, and whose work often functioned symbolically. Cosimo's family members represented various forces in Italian society after the Second World War, with Battista, the mad sister, embodying the Italian Communist Party. The party's attempts to dress up the horrors of Stalinism as delicious delicacies is made visible in her cooking. This was a resonant topic for Calvino, who fought alongside the communist partisans in Italy against the Fascists and the Nazis, but decided to resign his party membership in 1952 because of his disgust for the Soviet Union, which he described as 'a tragic and ferocious system'.

Those who want to know about Calvino's attitudes towards food are forced to scan his work, because one of his big ideas was the personal irrelevance of the writer. In the introduction to *Italo Calvino: Letters 1941–1985*, published in English in 1998, editor Michael Wood writes that Calvino was 'discreet about his life and the lives of others' and that he 'was inclined to think that a writer's work is all the biography anyone really requires'. Calvino himself said that 'For the critic, the author does not

Those who want to know about Calvino's attitudes towards food are forced to scan his work, because one of the writer's big ideas was the personal irrelevance of the writer.

exist, only a certain number of writings exist.' This was an early version of the idea of the 'death of the author' which Roland Barthes popularized in 1967 in an essay of that name.

Calvino, who worked for most of his life as an editor at the Italian publishing house Einaudi, was married and lived in his later years between Rome, Paris and Turin. He also had a country house on the Tuscan coast north of Grosseto. His translator described all Calvino's homes as giving the impression of being sparsely furnished; the writer himself said that he came from an 'austere' family. We also know from a rare interview published in *The Paris Review* that he did the shopping for his family ('buying bread, meat or fruit'), and that he found it difficult to settle down to writing-work in the mornings, which tended to be full of distractions – the newspapers, domestic tasks, errands – and only really put pen to paper in the afternoons.

The tree-nut tart above, inspired by *The Baron in the Trees,* is a tribute to Cosimo's decision to live forever in the tree-tops – symbolic, for Calvino, of choosing principles and the life of the mind over worldly concerns. It also pays tribute to a biographical note from Calvino's life: his father, an agronomist, studied the cultivation of fruit trees, and was a pioneer grower of both grapefruit and avocado trees in Italy. And though Calvino's personal life was austere, his intellectual life was lavish. To name just a few trees in the baron's domain: oak, mulberry, magnolia, apple, lemon, fig, cherry, quince, peach, almond, pear, plum, service, carob, walnut, olive, pine, larch, plane. What a fabulous array!

Andrea Camilleri

1925–2019

Detective novels clued in on Sicilian food

Sardines *a beccafico*

Serves 6 (as a side)
• 12 sardines, butterflied and heads, spines and bones removed, tails left on (you can ask your fishmonger to do this) • 3 tbsp olive oil, plus extra for greasing • 30g (1oz/½ cup) dried breadcrumbs • 2 tbsp pine nuts • 2 tbsp dried currants • 1 tbsp finely chopped parsley • About 6 bay leaves • Juice of 1 lemon • Juice of 1 orange • 2 tsp sugar • Salt and black pepper

Preheat the oven to 180°C/350°F/gas 4 and lightly oil a 20 x 15cm (8 x 6in) glass baking dish.

Lay out the sardines on a plate and season with salt and pepper.

Add 2 tablespoons of the olive oil to a small skillet and fry the breadcrumbs, stirring regularly, until browned. Add the pine nuts, currants and parsley, and season to taste.

Lay out a sardine, placing it skin side down, put a tablespoon of filling at the thickest end and roll it up toward the tail. Place it in the baking dish with the tail sticking up in the air. Repeat this to fill the rest of the sardines, and place them in the dish, alternating them with bay leaves and arranging them in neat rows so that they have no room to unroll.

Sprinkle the sardines with the juices of the lemon and orange, the sugar and the final tablespoon of olive oil. Bake for 25 minutes until the sardines are cooked and the filling is piping hot. Serve cold.

– Adapted from a recipe by Valerie Stivers for *The Paris Review*

Sicilian writer Andrea Camilleri is one of Italy's most famous and beloved authors, though his creation, Inspector Montalbano, has greater name-recognition than the author does outside of Italy. Camilleri also has an inspiring life story. He was a writer for television and of minor historical novels until 1994, when in his late sixties he published the first of Montalbano's adventures, *The Shape of Water*. The dashing Montalbano is a police inspector in Sicily, with a life of many complications: paperwork, corrupt officials, a jealous girlfriend, frequent corpses. Aggressive and tightly wound, the inspector does his job well, but takes frequent breaks to enjoy the incredible cuisine of his native island, a habit that also reflects Sicilian culture's formal, three-sit-down-meals-a-day approach to dining.

The Sicilian regional specialities on the pages of the Montalbano novels (there are twenty-eight with the last published in 2020, after Camilleri's death) are seemingly endless. Sicily has a vast maritime bounty – at one point, Montalbano memorably eats a starter of grilled fish followed by a second course of a different grilled fish. The island also specializes in farming and animal husbandry and has a distinctive cheesemaking tradition: ricotta, pecorino, a hanging bulb-shaped cheese called caciocavallo, are just a few. The wealth of its desserts hints at the island's history as a cosmopolitan hub of medieval Europe: cassata cake, gelato, marzipan pastry, cannoli, an extraordinary variety of named cookies, and more. A reader taking notes on the dishes in Montalbano novels could make pages of lists of mostly unfamiliar items, including things like the inspector's favourite snack of *càlia e simenza* (a mixture of roasted chickpeas and salted pumpkin seeds, eaten out of a paper cone) and the sardines *a beccafico* (above) that in one book cause him to wake with indigestion after having 'bolted down' too many the night before.

Camilleri kept a house in Sicily but mostly lived and worked in an apartment on a high floor of a building in a wealthy section of Rome. He was a heavy smoker and his elegant apartment was lined with books. He told *The Guardian*

The Sicilian regional specialities on the pages of the Montalbano novels are seemingly endless.

newspaper in 2012 that Inspector Montalbano's food habits did not mean he was greedy, but were a necessary counterbalance to his work as a detective. 'It's the same in the books of Simenon where Maigret is a man who loves good food,' Camilleri said. 'I think it is a sort of unconscious revenge of vitality, an affirmation of being alive in the face of continuous death. Maybe eating subconsciously expresses the pleasure of feeling alive. A life-force.' Camilleri also believed that by evoking a place in all its specifics – including its food – he could address larger themes. In an interview with *La Voce di New York*, he said, 'I remembered Dostoevsky's phrase: "Tell the story of your village. If you tell it well, you will have told the story of the world."'

Truman Capote

1924–84

'Food. I seldom think of anything else.'

Plaza Hotel Chicken Hash

• 4 Cups finely diced cooked chicken (white meat only) • 1 ½ C heavy cream • 1 C cream sauce (bechamel) • 2 tsps salt • ⅛ tsp white pepper • ¼ C dry Sherry • ½ C Hollandaise Sauce

Mix chicken, cream, Cream Sauce, and seasonings in a heavy skillet. Cook over moderate heat, stirring often for about 10 minutes. When moisture is slightly reduced, place skillet in a moderate oven 350 and bake 30 minutes. Stir in Sherry and return to oven for 10 minutes. Lightly fold in Hollandaise Sauce and serve at once. Makes 4–5 servings.

—From *Party of the Century: The Fabulous Story of Truman Capote and His Black and White Ball* by Deborah Davis

From the moment Truman Capote published his first novel, *Other Voices, Other Rooms*, in 1948, its languid, come-hither author photo, which looked openly homoerotic in an era when that was controversial, made him a national celebrity. The flamboyant boy from Alabama whose childhood best friend was the young Harper Lee would become a muse for Andy Warhol, friend of the international jet-set and confidant of New York's most beautiful A-List women. (Friends like Babe Paley, Slim Keith and Lee Radziwill have recently been returned to the public consciousness by the second season of the *Feud* television show, based on the writer's life, 'Capote vs. The Swans'.) In the course of a long career in the public eye, Capote answered many questions about his personal life, including about his diet. He was known for his stylish bon mots, and once said, 'Food. I seldom think of anything else.'

Much of what he liked was the kind of food served in the glamorous, high-society circles he frequented. His favourite place to dine was New York City's Plaza Hotel, also the venue for the defining social event of the 1960s, Capote's Black and White Ball, where guests included Lady Bird Johnson, Frank Sinatra and Mia Farrow. Capote frequently dined on the Plaza's creamy and decadent white chicken hash (above), an elevated version of a corned-beef hash. He's also on the record for preferring his baked potatoes with sour cream and black caviar, and provided the recipe for this dish twice, once to *Vogue* magazine and once to a charity cookbook designed for a school in Bridgehampton, New York, on Long Island's toney East End. For *Vogue* he suggested the potato be consumed with a quarter-pound of caviar and half a bottle of ice-cold champagne per person; in the Hamptons he recommended an accompaniment of chilled 80 proof Russian vodka.

Capote also sometimes celebrated the homey, Southern foods of his childhood. In November of 1968, he sat for photographs with *Ladies' Home Journal* for a story recreating the feast from his 1967 short story, *The Thanksgiving Visitor*. The original story describes a Thanksgiving with five turkeys and all the trimmings: home-canned vegetables, sweet potato casserole with raisins, 'ambrosia' of orange slices sprinkled with coconut, and cold banana pudding. The magazine loaded the table for its recreation with more Thanksgiving classics: pumpkin pie, 'olives with celery' (leafy celery stalks standing straight up in a dish of olives), biscuits, cornbread, cranberry-orange relish, home-made chocolates, and a tart apple cider. Another magazine, *Best Life*, found and published the cherry pie recipe allegedly used by Nancy Clutter and referred to in Capote's 1965 'nonfiction novel' masterpiece, *In Cold Blood*.

Capote himself did not often cook – from the time he could afford one, he always had a personal chef. But he did try his hand in the kitchen while living in Sicily with partner Jack Dunphy in the 1950s. There, he rented the same house D.H. Lawrence had lived in twenty-five years earlier. His many letters to friends and editors (gathered in 2004's *Too Brief a Treat: The Letters of Truman Capote)*, addressed affectionately to 'Magnolia love' or 'Darling – Precious – Lamb' or 'Light of the World', reveal a homey, cosy and happy Capote. His biographer and the editor of his letters, Gerald Clarke, refers to him as 'a loving friend, a zestful gossip, a buoyant spirit', who was especially suited to this period. In Sicily, Capote made preserves in old gin bottles, mentioning tomato, fig, apricot and peach, and also asked his correspondents for recipes for dishes like mayonnaise and chocolate pie. 'Must do something with all these old gin and wine bottles,' he wrote to Andrew Lyndon ('darling baby') in July of 1950. A few days later he writes that he's making lime meringue pies, 'practically every other day: Jack screams when I go near the kitchen'. And in November 'I wrestled with a Thanksgiving dinner and it came out pretty well'. Cooking, he wrote, is 'an unmanly activity, I suppose, but very relaxing and the reward is delicious'.

Miguel de Cervantes

1547–1616

Physical versus spiritual nourishment

Shepherd's Breadcrumbs

Serves 2

• ½ small (about 450g/1lb) loaf of good-quality bread, stale • ½ yellow onion, diced • ½ red (bell) pepper, deseeded and sliced • 4 tbsp olive oil • 1 garlic clove, minced • 115g (4oz) cured chorizo or diced pancetta • Salt and black pepper • A handful of green grapes, sliced, to serve

Tear or cut the bread into roughly 1cm (½in) square chunks. Sprinkle the bread with water until moist throughout but not soaked, then wrap in a damp dishtowel. Set aside.

In a pan on medium–high heat, sauté the onion and red pepper in the olive oil, stirring regularly, until the onion is translucent and the pepper has slightly wilted. Add the garlic and the chorizo or pancetta and cook until fragrant – about 2 minutes. Add the bread and cook on a low heat, stirring occasionally, until the bread is beginning to crisp. Season with salt and pepper to taste, then serve garnished with the sliced green grapes.

– Valerie Stivers

'What fried breadcrumbs, what cream cheeses, what garlands and shepherd's knickknacks!' exclaimed Sancho Panza, literature's first sidekick, in *Don Quixote*. 'They may not make me the name of a wise one, but they won't fail to get me a name for wit.' Panza is dreaming of his retirement from Quixote's service, when he imagines he'll work as a shepherd and eat well. And the dish he's referring to, *migas del pastor*, is a common one in rural Spain, made from the humble and ubiquitous ingredients of bread, garlic, water and salt, plus whatever else a shepherd might have on hand: an onion, red pepper, fresh or dried, some pancetta or chorizo. A regional twist in La Mancha, where Quixote is from, is to add a few green grapes.

Very little is known about Quixote's creator, early modern Spanish author Miguel de Cervantes – no portrait has been authenticated, and even his name is in question. He was born around 1547; his early life was spent in poverty and obscurity; he served in the Spanish navy and was captured by Barbary pirates in 1575, with whom he was enslaved for five years before being ransomed and returned to Madrid. However, *Don Quixote*, published in two parts in 1605 and 1615, is widely considered to be the first novel of the modern era and one of the most influential works of the Western literary canon. And it's full of food, which, according to Cervantes' translator and scholar B.W. Ife, does important work towards developing the book's themes.

La Mancha is an agricultural region on a high plateau in central Spain, which in Cervantes' time was known for its rustic society and traditional windmills, making it a satirical location for his knight-errant protagonist to be from. People from La Mancha are called Manchegos, and the region produces sheep, goats, grain, wine, and the hard and tangy sheep's milk cheese known as Manchego. The book's characters eat many of the local specialities. In a paper published on the website of King's College London, Ife explains that Quixote's staple diet before going on his quest consisted of the following elements: '"olla", by which we may assume is meant the classic slow-cooked stew made with beans and sausages known as "olla podrida", eaten as the main midday meal; "salpicon" or cold meat sliced thinly with onions and vinegar for supper; "lantejas" or lentils on Fridays; "duelos y quebrantos", probably some form of omelette, on Saturdays; and the occasional pigeon on Sundays.'

Don Quixote is an idealist and dreamer whose mind has been corrupted by reading too many of the popular books of the era – medieval tales of chivalry. Sancho Panza, his foil, is a down-to-earth working man and realist. To suit his impractical, head-in-the-clouds character, Quixote is thin, and neither eats nor sleeps much, whereas Panza, the realist, is fat and always thinking about food – a sensible man, in other words, who enjoys life. Quixote's lack of attention to food is one of the ways that Cervantes establishes his character's lack of interest in reality. Ife also points out that Quixote's diet may have been a reason for his delusions: he was malnourished. Moreover, Ife says that the *duelos y quebrantos* that Quixote ate on Saturdays was traditionally made with brains, the consumption of which could lead to bovine spongiform encephalopathy; Cervantes wouldn't have known that, but the people at the time correctly thought that eating brains could drive you mad.

And when Quixote hits the road, his delusions lead to even more hunger and poor sleeping. At the first inn he visits, which he mistakes for a castle, he refuses to take off his helmet and thus cannot eat any of the food on offer. Eventually the landlord brings him a straw so he can have a little bit to drink. Ife points out that it's only *after* not having eaten all day that Quixote makes the irrational choice to sit up all night watching his armour. So the lightheadedness and hallucinations he experiences make perfect sense. Nonetheless, in the larger sweep of the book's themes, Quixote's fate is not entirely a tragic one. In some sense his dreams and ideals are a noble separation of the character from the world, and he finds spiritual nourishment on his quest.

Paulo Coelho

1947–present

Beyond 'food and water'

Cook. Cooking is the most beautiful and most complete of the arts. It involves all our five senses, plus one more – the need to give of our best.

– From *Adultery* by Paulo Coelho

'I am much more like a rock star than a writer,' Paulo Coelho told the English writer and critic A.N. Wilson over lunch in 2010, referring to the unmanageable crowds he draws at book-signings. The Brazilian novelist was the second best-selling author in the world in the early 2000s, his work an unstoppable juggernaut that started with the global hit *The Alchemist*, first published in 1988. It is the story of an Andalusian shepherd boy's trek across North Africa in search of a great treasure, which symbolically suggests a quest for spiritual fulfilment. On his blog, Coelho explains his magic writing formula is to use 'complex symbolism to depict the journeys' of his characters, who are 'typically motivated by spiritual beliefs'. His topics are 'love, self-awareness, sexual desire, solitude, chasing one's dreams, and traveling'. And his books succeed because they 'satisfy the soul'.

Coelho is a man who understands satisfaction, and whose wisdom and thoughts on life have connected with untold millions of people, so it's fascinating to see how such an insightful and influential person approaches food. Naturally, as a writer Coelho has a talent for aphorisms, and he often issued food-related ones for his 14.9 million followers on X (formerly Twitter). One that comes up from February 2018: 'Memories are like salt: the right amount brings out the flavor in food, too much ruins it.' Another frequently quoted soundbite is: 'Dreams nourish the soul just as food nourishes the body.' In *The Alchemist*, the higher needs of the shepherd boy to dream and accomplish a life's purpose are contrasted with the simple needs of his sheep for basic 'food and water'.

But when it comes to how Coelho actually eats, he strikes what sounds like a down-to-earth balance between pleasure and good health. Coelho is slim, trim and vigorous for his age, and he celebrates simple food, good food and eating for pleasure, at the same time as he doesn't over-eat. In an interview with *The Guardian* in 2003, he says, 'I enjoy my meals and stay healthy by not being in a hurry and making them into a celebration. I hate this food fundamentalism which is becoming a collective sickness in our world. We are losing tasty food and exchanging it for boring, healthy dishes.' When he eats at home with his wife, it's a practical business of 'feeding ourselves', he says, but when they go out, it's 'more of a ritual when we can have time together'. He tells the paper that his breakfast is a simple 'black coffee, fresh orange juice, and a French roll with olive oil'. During the day he likes 'a ham sandwich or plain boiled rice'. Dinner is at seven o'clock. When in Brazil, he eats a classic Brazilian stew of black bean, rice, flour and beef; when abroad he goes out to eat, splurging on foie gras or a sirloin steak. He also has dessert every day (he especially likes coffee ice cream) and drinks a bottle of Bordeaux over dinner with his wife. He believes that 'Food should taste of itself. There should not be too much embellishment.' His favourite food of all is bread.

A.N. Wilson saw this philosophy in action during a *Financial Times* interview in 2003 during Coelho's promotional tour for his book *Inspirations: Selections from Classic Literature*. Wilson met Coelho over lunch at the five-star Restaurant-Hôtel du Parc des Eaux-Vives, in Geneva, Switzerland. The critic-journalist was looking forward to an elaborate French-influenced meal, perhaps the pig's cheeks with sage or medallions of Maine lobster, but Coelho ate only a simple boiled egg. After the meal, Wilson observed him jogging home.

Writers' Favourite Cocktails

Evelyn Waugh: The Stinger

An upper crust tipple

• 50ml (1.75fl oz) cognac • 20ml (0.75fl oz) creme de menthe

Shake over ice and pour into a glass, neat

F. Scott Fitzgerald: Gin Rickey

The drink of a jazz age icon

• 60ml (2fl oz) gin • Juice of ½ lemon • Top with club soda

Serve in a highball glass

Rex Stout: Montenegro After Dark

A detective writer's exotic sip

• 60ml (2fl oz) Amaro Montenegro •15ml (0.5fl oz) bourbon •15ml (0.5fl oz) mezcal • 1 tbsp sugar syrup • 2 dashes orange bitters • 1 dash Angostura aromatic bitters

Mix and serve over ice

William Faulkner: Mint Julep

The taste of the American South

• 120ml (4fl oz) bourbon • ¼ cup mint syrup • Sprig of mint to top

Serve over ice

Jean-Paul Sarte & Simone De Beauvoir: Apricot Fuzzy Naval

The drink that inspired existentialism

• 90ml (3fl oz) apricot schnapps or apricot brandy • 90ml (3fl oz) orange juice • Orange slices for garnish

Mix and serve over ice

Eve Babitz: The Bloody Mary

The LA sexpot's slurp

• 120ml (4fl oz) tomato juice • 45ml (1.5fl oz) vodka • 1 tbsp lemon juice • 2 dashes Worcestershire Sauce • Salt and pepper • Celery stick to garnish

Serve over ice in a highball glass

E.B. White: Gin Martini

He drank them like others take aspirin

• 150ml (5fl oz) 94% proof good English gin, preferably Beefeater or Tanquerey • 1½ capfuls Noilly Prat or Martini & Rossi dry vermouth • 6–8 cubes hard ice, cracked by hand • 1 olive or 1 twist lemon peel

Pour over ice and shake

Decant in a martini glass, add olive or lemon twist and serve

(From *Life is Meals*, by James Salter & Kay Salter)

Anne Sexton & Sylvia Plath: Extra-Dry Martinis

The friends-and-rival poets had a three-martini lunch

• 15ml (0.5fl oz) vermouth • 60–90ml (2–3fl oz) gin or vodka • Lemon twist or olives to serve

Pour vermouth over ice in a shaker; stir, let sit 20 seconds and drain
Pour vodka into the same shaker; stir, let sit 20 seconds
Serve in a martini glass

Ernest Hemingway: Daiquiri

The recipe from his favourite Floridita Bar in Havana

• Juice of half a lime • 1 tsp sugar • 45ml (1.5fl oz) light rum • Dash of maraschino • 1 cup crushed ice

Shake, strain and serve
(From *Life is Meals*, by James Salter & Kay Salter)

Truman Capote: Screwdriver

He called it his 'orange drink'

• 1 part vodka • 2 parts orange juice

Serve over ice in a highball glass, with orange slice for garnish

Colette

1873–1954

A soul made from 'haricots beans and little strips of bacon'

Cherry Clafoutis

Serves 8

• Butter, for greasing • 350g (12oz) cherries • 3 eggs • 100g (3½oz/½ cup) sugar, plus extra for the dish • ½ tsp vanilla extract • 1 tbsp kirsch • A pinch of salt • 65g (2¼oz/½ cup) plain (all-purpose) flour • 240ml (8fl oz/1 cup) milk • 60ml (2fl oz/¼ cup) double (heavy) cream • Icing (confectioners') sugar, for dusting

Preheat the oven to 190°C/375°F/gas 5. Butter and sugar a 23cm (9in) round ceramic pie plate with 5cm (2in) sides. Spread the cherries out in the pie plate.

In the bowl of an electric mixer, beat together the eggs, sugar, vanilla extract, kirsch, salt, flour, milk and cream on medium speed until well combined. Pour the batter over the cherries.

Bake until a thin knife inserted near the centre of the clafoutis comes out clean and the top is a deep golden colour – about 40 minutes. If the top is brown before the custard is done, loosely cover with a sheet of foil.
Place the dish on a wire rack to cool a little, but serve warm. Just before serving, dust the top of the clafoutis with icing sugar, and serve in either scoops or wedges.

– Adapted from a recipe by Valerie Stivers for *The Paris Review*

'My soul is full of nothing but haricot beans and little strips of bacon,' the Colette heroine Claudine tells a young literary man trying to seduce her in the 1902 novel *Claudine en ménage,* perfectly encapsulating the *fin de siècle* French writer's sensual and pragmatic attitude towards life. Colette was born Sidonie-Gabrielle Colette to a middle-class family in the poor part of Burgundy in 1873. In her early teens, possessor of a lithe body, cat-like green eyes and braids that reached her ankles, she captured the attention of a nobleman friend of her father's, Henry Gauthier-Villars, a publishing impresario who ran a Paris workshop pumping out novels, articles and music criticism under the pen-name 'Willy'. Over the objections of his family, they married in 1893 when she was twenty. Willy brought her to Paris, where he encouraged her to write the first of the Claudine novels, *Claudine a l'ecole*, a semi-erotic tale of a schoolgirl discovering her sexuality. As she wrote in a confessional work in 1936, quoted by biographer Judith Thurman in *Secrets of the Flesh: A Life of Colette*, girls at this age suffer 'the neuroses of puberty, the habit of eating clay and charcoal, of drinking mouthwash, of reading dirty books, and sticking pins into the palm'. Thurman credits Colette with having 'invented the century's first teenage girl'.

Colette published under Willy's name for her first several books, but separated from him in 1906, going on to become an impecunious stage performer who often went hungry, and later turning once again to writing to make her living. In time she became one of the most famous women in French letters, a tireless producer of articles, essays, novels, non-fiction, reminiscences and more, whose sex life was also scandalous news – she slept with women, seduced her second husband's teenage son, and later married a much younger man, Maurice Goudeket.

Colette's true passion, however, was food. A *New York Times* story from 1979 quotes her as once having 'happily' said, '*Je suis gourmette, gourmande, gloutonne.*' (I am a gourmet, a gourmande and a glutton.) Her friend, the author Violet Trefusis, quoted on the Nick Harvill Libraries blog, claimed that Colette was 'cozy. She loved mixing the sauce vinaigrette that accompanied her home-grown salad; her kitchen was more familiar to her than her drawing room. She adored comfort and disdained luxury . . . Especially she disliked women whose conversation was as skimpy as their diet.' Another anecdote reported by Thurman has Colette teasing a group of learned and religious men gathered to discuss morality in literature. A contemporary recording the scene wrote: 'She talked cooking and Château d'Yquem, and the dishes one could serve with it. She brings everything down to gourmandise: the greed for food, the greed for sensual pleasure. She kept repeating that purity is a temptation like the others, and not a nobler one.'

The effortless culinary details in Colette's novels also reveal a woman who understood food and liked to eat. In *Gigi*, a late novella that is one of her most popular, the rustic French dish of cassoulet appears as a set-piece: Colette's scheming provincial characters serve it to a wealthy nobleman who is being tricked into marrying a beautiful and seemingly innocent teenage girl. The girl is supposedly as homespun as the humble cassoulet, but in fact she is shrewdly selling herself, much like the young Colette may have done. Elsewhere, Colette's eponymous hero Julie in *Julie de Carneilhan*, a middle-aged woman down on her luck, eats 'a cold pork cutlet, a slice of bread and butter, half a pound of red currants and a cup of excellent coffee' for a lunch that she considers too small and unsatisfying. For dinner there is hot chocolate and a slice of rye bread 'folded in a rough silk Turkish napkin'. She is down but not out, and even in duress she wants to enjoy herself.

Colette's food is wonderful but no-nonsense, as she was herself. She loved shellfish, and dessert in her work is most often fresh fruit or a 'simple cake'. The clafoutis recipe above is a classic French dessert that combines both.

Laurie Colwin

1944–92

She washed dishes in the bathtub

Gingerbread with Chocolate Icing

Cream one stick of sweet butter with ½ cup light or dark brown sugar. Beat until fluffy and add ½ cup molasses.

Beat in two eggs.

Add 1½ cups of flour, ½ teaspoon of baking soda and one very generous tablespoon of ground ginger (this can be adjusted to taste, but I like it very gingery). Add one teaspoon of cinnamon, ¼ teaspoon of ground cloves and ¼ teaspoon of ground allspice.

Add two teaspoons of lemon brandy. If you don't have any use plain vanilla extract. *Lemon extract will not do.* Then add ½ cup of buttermilk (or milk with a little yogurt beaten into it) and turn batter into a buttered tin. Bake at 350 for between twenty and thirty minutes (check after twenty minutes have passed). Test with a broom straw, and cool on a rack.

Chocolate Icing

Cream ½ stick of sweet butter. When fluffy add four tablespoons of unsweetened cocoa.

If you have some, add one teaspoon of vanilla brandy (easily made by steeping a couple of cut-up vanilla beans in brandy – another excellent thing to have around), or plain vanilla or plain brandy. Then add about a cup of powdered sugar, a little at a time until you get the consistency you want.

– From *Home Cooking* by Laurie Colwin

Laurie Colwin's novel *Family Happiness* features a scene where a mother and daughter get on the telephone to discuss the menu for an upcoming family dinner – a roast leg of lamb or roast beef, with potatoes and, as the mother says, 'those lovely cold string beans of yours for a second vegetable'. Colwin writes: 'On both sides of the line, mother and daughter settled down for the conversation they enjoyed most: what to serve with what for dinner.' The two agree to decorate the table with quince branches and have apple pie for dessert. The scene is quintessentially Colwin: it's relatable, since many mothers and daughters discuss dinner menus, but glamorous too – those quince branches . . . It creates an intense nostalgia for a kind of idealized family life that few people really experience. And it's about food.

Colwin wrote five novels and enough essays for two collections of food writing before her death in 1992 at age forty-eight from an aortic aneurysm. Despite her early death, she has remained in print as a reader-favourite in the domestic and the romantic-comedy genre, and all her books were reissued in 2021. Both her adult child, RF Jurjevics, and longtime friend Willard Spiegelman say that her two interests – fiction and food – were really two facets of an overriding interest in people. She loved to bring people together for dinner, talk to them and get their life story. 'Laurie often had people in the kitchen before a meal, and she would often start her inquiries there,' Jurjevics told me. 'My father told me that [he] knew Laurie was going to begin in earnest [when] she would ask her subject, re: their romantic partner, "*so*: how did you two meet?"'

Colwin's style, in life and in fiction, was a response to her family and childhood. She was born to Jewish parents in Manhattan, but the family moved around a lot and lived in various suburbs during her formative years, which she hated. Colwin's mother, Jurjevics says, was 'very difficult'. She was a grande dame who served dinner with crystal and had an interest in social climbing, according to Spiegelman, and her

She extolled the virtues of simple, everyday food made luxurious and fun through the occasional high-quality ingredient or in-the-know cooking technique.

relationship with her daughter was 'fractious'. Colwin, by contrast, valued casualness, haphazardness and warmth in her social life. After a few unhappy years at college she dropped out and struck out on her own, living in New York City on a shoestring as a struggling writer, and throwing frequent dinner parties that were notable for their lack of pretension.

Colwin's first apartment in New York was a studio that had only a two-burner electric hot-plate to cook on, and no kitchen sink. In *Home Cooking*, her first collection of food writing, she confesses that in this apartment she 'did the dishes in a plastic pan in the bathtub and set the dish drainer over the toilet'. When she had people over, she set up a card table 'with a cigarette burn in its leatherette top' as a dinner table. Her columns for *Gourmet* magazine (collected in *Home Cooking*) extolled the virtues of simple, everyday food made luxurious and fun through the occasional high-quality ingredient or in-the-know cooking technique. She wrote recipes for beef stew and chicken salad and eschewed kitchen gadgetry – an informal approach for a girl who grew up dining on crystal. The gingerbread recipe above has a similar ersatz inspiration: Colwin originally made the cake using the miniature baking trays from Jurjevics's toy kitchen.

Mars
WONKA
KitKat

Roald Dahl

1916–90

A Kit Kat on his writing desk

Frozen Chocolate Kit Kat Cake

Serves 10

For the chocolate ganache:

• 110g (4oz) good bittersweet chocolate • 150ml (½ cup) heavy cream • ½ tablespoon butter

For the cake:

• 300ml (1 cup) heavy cream • 1 tablespoon sugar • 54 rectangular wafer cookies (like Loacker)

Make the ganache: Place the chocolate in a microwave-safe bowl and microwave for 30 seconds. Stir, and continue to microwave in 10 second increments until melted. In a small saucepan, bring the cream to a simmer. Remove from heat, add melted chocolate and butter, and stir until smooth. Set aside.

Using an electric mixer, beat the cream and 1 tbsp sugar on medium speed until soft peaks form. Line a large plate with parchment paper.

Assemble the cake: Use 6 wafers to create a large rectangle on the parchment-lined plate. Spread on a layer of ganache, then top with another 6 wafers. Add another layer of ganache, followed by a ¼in layer of whipped cream. Continue assembling in this order – wafer, ganache, wafer, ganache, whipped cream – until all the wafers are gone. Top with ganache, allowing extra to run over the sides. Freeze for at least four hours, until ganache has set, then cut and serve immediately.

– Valerie Stivers

Roald Dahl loved sweets, especially chocolate, and double-especially Kit Kats. As an adult, the creator of the 1964 children's classic *Charlie and the Chocolate Factory* ate a Kit Kat a day, and made a giant silver ball of their foil to use as a paperweight, which sat on his writing desk. When he was a child in the 1920s, however, as he put it in *Roald Dahl's Cookbook*, 'the great golden years of the chocolate revolution had not yet begun' and the 'small boys and girls' were stuck with 'sherbet-suckers and gobstoppers and licorice bootlaces and aniseed balls'. Oh no!

Dahl went away to boarding school when he was seven years old, where he discovered that teachers and older students could freely deliver terrible beatings or be psychologically cruel to those who were less powerful. His school experience was so awful, he wrote later, that it made him lose his faith in God, and also inspired the loathing of bullying and cruelty that runs through his works for children. One bright spot at school was the occasional mystery box from Cadbury, which the chocolatier sent for the boys to critique the experimental wares it had begun developing.

Young Roald dreamed of the fabulous workshop where the sweets were being made – it must have been a needed escape from the conditions at school – and later those dreams became the inspiration for Willy Wonka's lair. The experience must have also cemented his lifelong commitment to sweets. His second wife Felicity (known as Liccy) reveals in the cookbook they wrote together that he kept a jar of wine gums beside the bed for midnight snacking. And Sophie Dahl, his granddaughter, fondly recalls a 'magic' red Tupperware box that he would bring out at the end of lunch or dinner that contained 'chocolate. Lots of chocolate, in appealing child-sized bars, nothing fancy but always compelling.'

Nonetheless, Dahl was suspicious of gluttony, which is often a characteristic of his villains. Augustus Gloop, a rude and greedy boy in *Charlie and the Chocolate Factory,* meets his untimely fate after sneaking down to Willy Wonka's chocolate river and 'scooping hot melted chocolate into his mouth as fast as he could . . . "This stuff is *tee*-riffic,"' he says. '"Oh boy, I need a bucket to drink it properly!"' The awful Aunt Sponge in *James and the Giant Peach* is described as being 'enormously fat and very short. She had small piggy eyes, a sunken mouth, and one of those white, flabby faces that looked exactly as though it had been boiled.' The equating of being fat with being bad has become culturally dated, but Dahl intended it to convey that the character was selfish and greedy – traits that his work spoke out against.

Dahl felt that enjoyment of good food, well-prepared and in the right measure, was fine, however, and he celebrated it as one of life's great pleasures. (Charlie, remember, is rewarded with a lifetime's supply of chocolate at the end of the book.) Dahl wrote one cookbook (now available under the title *Roald Dahl's Cookbook)*, a joint project with Liccy published posthumously in 1991, and left notes for another, *Roald Dahl's Revolting Recipes*, a book for children based on the wonderful and disgusting foods in his work, which Liccy completed after his death. The former offers the greatest hits from Dahl's dining room at Gipsy House, his longtime home in the village of Great Missenden in Buckinghamshire: recipes for Grilled Lobsters in Hot Herb Butter or Latticed Lamb and Apricot Roulade with Onion Sauce are accompanied by family anecdotes, wisdom on topics such as how best to eat vegetables – only when freshly picked, if you can – and a lengthy history of chocolate, penned by Dahl himself. *Revolting Recipes*' Hot Frogs, Lickable Wallpaper, Wormy Spaghetti and Fresh Mudburgers are a disappointment (hint: the spaghetti does not have worms in it; the mudburgers are just burgers). Above is a recipe for something more delicious: a Kit Kat-inspired cake a little smaller than the Giant Peach, but still quite impressive.

Charles Dickens

1812–70

Food for emotional comfort

Leg of Mutton Stuffed with Oysters

Parboil some fine well-fed oysters, take off the beards and horny parts, put to them some parsley, minced onions, and sweet herbs boiled and chopped fine, and the yolks of two or three hard-boiled eggs: mix all together, and make five or six holes in the fleshy part of a leg of mutton, and put in the mixture, and dress it in either of the following ways; tie it up in a cloth and let it boil gently two and a half or three hours according to the size, or braise it and serve it with pungent brown sauce.

– From *What Shall We Have for Dinner?* by Catherine Dickens, as reproduced in *Dinner With Dickens* by Pen Vogler

With the words 'Please, sir, I want some more', the orphan Oliver Twist became one of the most beloved characters in literature, and it's characteristic of Charles Dickens' work that this iconic scene involves food. Dickens was 'fascinated by what connected people', according to Pen Vogler, author of the cookbook *Dinner With Dickens*, 'and he dramatizes the material relationship [between people] . . . through the food his characters give, share, steal or long for'.

For example, in *Great Expectations*, the orphan Pip brings a meal to an escaped convict that will change the course of Pip's life. The convict encounters Pip playing on the gloomy marshes between a graveyard and a prison on the Kent coastline, and demands that he return home and steal food for him. Pip, terrified, does so: bread, a rind of cheese, half a jar of mincemeat, brandy, a meat bone and 'a beautiful round compact pork pie'. Slowly over the course of the novel it becomes clear just how much this feast signifies about Pip's character: he didn't just steal food, he stole the most and the best food he could come up with. He was acting under pressure, afraid for his life, but unwittingly his choices were an expression of a hard-working, intelligent and generous spirit. And they meant an enormous amount to the starving convict, as plot developments later make clear.

Dickens isn't in literary fashion the way he used to be. Some think his techniques, such as deliberately exaggerated supporting characters and slapstick comedy routines, are contrary to the prevailing literary realism of our era. If so, it's a shame because he beautifully depicts the basic human desire for comfort through human connection – often symbolized by food – and this remains a vibrant, universal topic. Of all writers, Dickens sometimes seems to have the greatest generosity of spirit, and the most fundamental grasp of what's important in life.

The writer's wisdom was gained the hard way, through personal experience of early privation, including hunger. When Dickens was twelve years old, his father was locked up in the Marshalsea debtors' prison. Young Charles was forced to work for two years in a boot-blacking factory to help keep his family from destitution, and felt betrayed by his mother for events related to the experience. Vogler writes that 'his autobiographical novel *David Copperfield* shows not just the desperation of having an empty belly but also the ache for the consolation and security of being nourished by a loving parent'.

It's no wonder then that once he was rich and successful, Dickens kept a good table, nor that he believed strongly that 'domestic comfort and virtue' was an answer to many of society's ills, Vogler writes. Posterity has been left with a good deal of information about what the Dickenses ate,

thanks to a publication from 1852 entitled *What Should We Have for Dinner?* by the pseudonymous 'Lady Maria Clutterbuck'. The book was most likely written by Dickens' wife Catherine, with help from the writer himself. It offered 'bills of fare' for dinners of various sizes, from 'two or three persons' to 'fourteen, eighteen or twenty persons' – great party! – and included recipes using ingredients such as mutton, oysters, shrimp, raspberries, salad and macaroni. The leg of mutton stuffed with oysters, above, is from the book. Dickens also mentions the dish in *Little Dorrit*, and in a letter from November 1840 as something he'd eaten with a friend, so he must have liked it. Sweets are less well represented in the Dickens family cookbook: many of Catherine's menus end with 'toasted cheese' – possibly made in a special Victorian cheese-melting contraption that the Dickenses owned.

His fiction is full of condemnations of the people and organizations that contribute to others going hungry – including very often the organizations putatively set up to help the poor.

'Dickens delighted in sharing food with friends,' Vogler writes. 'His correspondence is littered with notes inviting people to dine at prompt hours – "at 1/4 before 7 o'clock".' He also worked with the philanthropists and social reformers of his era to help the hungry and needy. With heiress Angela Burdett-Coutts, he helped set up a home teaching 'fallen women . . . cookery and other domestic virtues', Vogler reports. And his fiction is full of condemnations of the people and organizations that contribute to others going hungry – often including the very organizations putatively set up to help the poor.

The ultimate shared meal in Victorian England, of course, took place at Christmas. And the Christmas meal from Dickens' 1843 classic *A Christmas Carol* remains the essence of the holiday. The Cratchits' meal isn't lavish, however – Dickens does not forget his roots. Their Christmas dinner starts with 'a mixture of gin and lemons' stirred 'round and round' and put 'on the hob to simmer'. The Christmas goose is so hotly anticipated that the children stuff spoons in their mouths 'lest they should shriek for goose before their turn came to be helped'. Once it has been served, its 'tenderness and flavour, size and cheapness were themes of universal admiration'. Beyond that, the Cratchits have only apple sauce and mashed potatoes, and remark on how the dinner was 'sufficient' for the whole family – faint praise until you recall that eating their fill is a treat. Dessert is a boiled pudding 'like a speckled cannon-ball' that nonetheless might be a little small for the family, though no one would say so, and roasted chestnuts. Fortunately, the book ends with the reformation of Bob Cratchit's employer, Ebenezer Scrooge, and a raise for Cratchit. In the future, the family will dine better at Christmas, and Scrooge will 'keep Christmas well' too, Dickens writes. Kindness to others and the enjoyment of a good meal go hand in hand.

Emily Dickinson

1830–86

She wrote poetry in the kitchen

Coconut Cake

• 1 pound sugar • ½ — butter • ½ — flour • ½ cup milk • 6 eggs • 1 grated cocoa nut

— From a note by Emily Dickinson, held at Amherst College Digital Collection

Baking and poetry are good pastimes for a recluse, and even have a few things in common, since in both cases the right balance of ingredients assembled in secret makes a new and perfect alchemy – cake, bread, muffin, words. Amherst's woman in white, Emily Dickinson, enjoyed both. The nineteenth-century author was the sheltered daughter of an educated and genteel family. Her grandfather, Samuel Dickinson, helped found Amherst College; her father, Edward Dickinson, served in the Massachusetts Senate and the Massachusetts House of Representatives, before becoming a US Congressman. Dickinson lived most of her life in her family home on Main Street in Amherst, now the Emily Dickinson Museum, and never married. In her later years she rarely left the house. But from within it she produced a stream of masterpieces.

'The fact of her seclusion and intellectual brilliancy was one of the familiar Amherst traditions,' her sister-in-law Susan Gilbert Dickinson wrote in her obituary. Still, it was a surprise when, after Dickinson's death, her family found forty manuscript books that Dickinson had created from 1858 to 1865 containing 800 poems whose existence no one had been aware of. During her lifetime, she was better known as a baker. To friend Abiah Root in September 1845, Dickinson wrote, 'I am going to learn to make bread tomorrow. So you may imagine me with my sleeves rolled up mixing Flour, Milk, Saleratus &c. with a deal of grace.' She was soon boasting that her bread was so good it was the only kind her father would eat. The poet also frequently sent care packages to friends or people who were ill or in need, and would sometimes include a pressed flower or poem among the gifts. She sent Susan, her dear friend and future sister-in-law, 'rice cake' and 'caramel rule' (chocolate caramel) when the latter was teaching in Baltimore, and said in a note: 'You thank me for the Rice cake – you tell me Susie, you have just been tasting it – and how happy I am to send you anything you love.' In another note – all of which are held at the Emily Dickinson Museum – she wrote that 'love's oven is warm'. Neighbourhood children loved her for her habit of lowering gingerbread down to them in a basket from a second floor window (done that way because she didn't like to leave the house).

To anyone who loves to bake, Dickinson's life sounds enjoyable indeed – she had so many creative things to do at home, she may not have *needed* to leave the house. Bakers will also recognize the creative inspiration she took from being in the kitchen and from food. She liked to eat, and in a letter to brother Austin in October of 1847, catalogued devouring a care package of 'cake – gingerbread – pie & peaches'. The 'apples – chestnuts & grapes still remain & will I hope for some time', she wrote. And she liked to use food metaphors in her poetry, such as one in which she compares 'surprise' to a pungent sauce 'Upon a tasteless meat'. Alone, the sauce would be 'too acrid – but combined /An edible Delight –'.

When baking, Dickinson sometimes scribbled poems on the back of recipes. A draft of the poem 'The Things that never can come back, are several –' (below) appears on the reverse of her recipe for coconut cake (above). Dickinson scholars suggest that the exotic cake ingredients may have inspired the poet's thoughts about journeys and travellers. There was also a poem scribbled on the back of a packet of Parisian baking chocolate. An article on the Emily Dickinson Museum website concludes that 'The many drafts of poems written on kitchen papers tell us also that this was a space of creative ferment for her, and that the writing of poetry mixed in her life with the making of delicate treats.'

In her poetry, Dickinson truly seemed to enjoy her life, and did not need to go far from home for an insight into the human condition. The following poem may seem to celebrate roaming, but returns home in the end.

The Things that never can come back, are several –
Childhood – some forms of Hope – the Dead –
Though Joys – like Men – may sometimes make a Journey –
And still abide –
We do not mourn for Traveler, or Sailor,
Their Routes are fair –
But think enlarged of all that they will tell us
Returning here –
'Here!' There are typic 'Heres' –
Foretold Locations –
The Spirit does not stand –
Himself – at whatsoever Fathom
His Native Land –

Joan Didion

1934–2021

She defined the California kitchen

Parsley Salad

(Serves 35–40)
8 bunches Italian parsley
Blend 16 T olive oil with one head parsley until smooth
Blend in 4 T balsamic vinegar, salt and pepper
When ready to serve place parsley in 1⅓ C grated parmesan in bowl, toss with dressing

– From a collection of Joan Didion's recipes, online at The Marginalian

During those five years I appeared, on the face of it, a competent enough member of some community or another . . . I . . . participated in the paranoia of the time, in the raising of a small child, and in the entertainment of large numbers of people passing through my house; made gingham curtains for spare bedrooms, remembered to ask agents if any reduction of points would be *pari passu* with the financing studio, put lentils in to soak Saturday night for lentil soup on Sunday . . .

– From *The White Album* by Joan Didion

Joan Didion was a recipe for California cool, one part propulsive, minimalist prose, and one part slim figure and stone-faced stare. Didion's essays, novels and journalism captured the discontent of the 1960s, and the loopy, lost feeling that comes over a person in the Golden State. But despite her detached persona, she was a super-achiever. She thought of herself as a novelist, but her most lasting books are probably both essay collections: *Slouching Towards Bethlehem* (1968) and *The White Album* (1979). And at the same time, during her greatest career-building years, she was cooking sit-down dinners for forty and mothering a little girl, her adopted daughter Quintana Roo Dunne.

Didion's domesticity was not exactly behind-the-scenes. As the first great female practitioner of New Journalism, Didion often wrote about her personal life, an act that feminized the literary myth of those times. But domesticity wasn't quite part of her persona, either. Her giant Le Creuset pots and lentil soups, like her tow-headed daughter and famous friends, are part of the background as her prose speeds by on its way to elsewhere – or perhaps to nowhere, as was her perennial fear. The writer Katie Roiphe noted in Didion's obituary in *The New York Times* that Didion's revelations were only 'seemingly' personal – it's an important qualification, since Didion was somehow both forthcoming and not, a cipher to the end.

Didion always made the domestic look off-hand. 'I remember taking a 25-mg. Compazine [a medication used to treat nausea, migraines, schizophrenia, psychosis and anxiety] one Easter Sunday and making a large and elaborate lunch for a number of people, many of whom were still around on Monday,' she wrote breezily in the title essay for *The White Album*. Or, attending a recording session for the band The Doors, she casually drops that there were 'paper bags half-filled with hard-boiled eggs and chicken livers and cheeseburgers and empty bottles of apple juice and California rosé'. (The rock-star life!) And in *Blue Nights*, the 2011 book she wrote about Quintana Roo's untimely early death, she quotes her husband John Gregory Dunne, also a writer, on her routine during Quintana's school days: 'Joan

was trying to finish a book that year, and she would work until two or three in the morning, then have a drink and read some poetry before she came to bed. She always made Q's lunch the night before, and put it in this little blue lunchbox. You should have seen those lunches . . . [t]hin little sandwiches with their crusts cut off, cut into four triangular pieces, kept fresh in Saran Wrap. Or else there would be homemade fried chicken with little salt and pepper shakers. And for dessert, stemmed strawberries, with sour cream and brown sugar.'

She always claimed that she learned to cook while she worked at *Vogue* magazine in New York in her twenties

For all that has been said about Didion's mordant, minimalist writing style, it's these blurry background glimpses of her wonderful world that have kept readers so passionately engaged with her work. A 2023 *Dwell* article devotes itself to an analysis of Didion's kitchen style, seen in photos from a 1972 *Vogue* shoot. The 'California kitchen' aesthetic, the writer explains, is 'a hodgepodge of French farmhouse, Craftsman, and Spanish Revival'. And Didion's enviable kitchen in her 'cliffside Malibu home' defines it. She has the French cookware, and the hanging baskets that the writer tells us are used for storing eggs in French farmhouse kitchens but here hold 'lemons, grapefruits, oranges, Vidalia onions, and garlic bulbs'. Underneath are 'three Mexican ceramic planters – presumably chipped and weathered by the salty breeze of the Pacific Ocean', for growing 'chives, mint' and a third herb the writer can't identify. Didion herself stands by, chopping leafy greens.

More cool details: Didion started her writing day with an ice-cold Coca-Cola for breakfast. She always claimed that she learned to cook while she worked at *Vogue* magazine in New York in her twenties – it was her job to proofread the recipes. And she made all kinds of meals for all kinds of people, many of them famous. Her nephew Griffin Dunne, director of the 2017 documentary *Joan Didion: The Center Will Not Hold*, assembled a cookbook from her recipe cards, menus and saved clippings, and distributed it as a

Kickstarter reward to promote financing of the documentary. Website The Marginalian has reproduced some of it online, including an image of a hand-written recipe for borscht (two pounds of stew beef; a highly specific 4.5 beets and ¾ of a cabbage). For Patti Smith, Didion made 'chicken hash with roasted yellow peppers and baguettes'; for Richard Roth, 'baked ham with mustard and Alice Waters's coleslaw'. The scale of her entertaining is revealed by that parsley salad for 35 to 40, above.

After Didion died, Stair Galleries in Hudson, New York, held an auction of her personal items, which turned into a cultural phenomenon. Writers from the city made 'pilgrimages' to see the auction house's small public display of Didion's things, according to one such pilgrim, Sophie Haigney, writing about the experience for *The Paris Review*. Haigney's trip was at least in part to understand the reasons for Didion's forever appeal. The writer has become a cultural 'relic', Haigney concludes, explaining that '[s]he came . . . to symbolize something, or a whole set of different and sometimes contradictory somethings, about being a writer, a woman, and a person of certain class at a certain time in America'.

When the auction started, 'it was clear quite quickly that, perhaps as expected, it was going to get out of hand', Haigney writes. 'Many of my friends were watching on and off all day, enjoying the spectacle in a corner of their screens at work, like they might once have watched the Comey hearings.' Didion's effects sold for amounts vastly over the starting price. One buyer spent $27,000 on the writer's Celine sunglasses. Napkins monogrammed JDD went for $14,000. And a rolling pin and aprons – relics of the California kitchen, at least in spirit – commanded $6,000. Didion didn't hand down a pie recipe that we know of, but that shouldn't stop the lucky buyer from putting on the apron and baking one.

Alexandre Dumas

1802–70

His true love was gastronomy

The Salad That So Fascinated Poor Ronconi

Finally, I made a salad that satisfied my guests so well that when Ronconi, one of my most regular guests, could not come he sent for his share of the salad, which was taken to him under a great umbrella when it rained so that no foreign matter might spoil it . . .

[This salad was] of great imagination, composite order, with five principal ingredients: Slices of beet, half-moons of celery, minced truffles, rampion with its leaves, and boiled potatoes . . .

First, I put the ingredients into the salad bowl, then overturn them onto a platter. Into the empty bowl I put one hard-boiled egg yolk for each two persons – six for a dozen guests. These I mash with oil to form a paste, to which I add chervil, crushed tuna, macerated anchovies, Maille mustard, a large spoonful of soya, chopped gherkins, and the chopped white of the eggs. I thin this mixture by stirring in the finest vinegar obtainable. Finally, I put the salad back into the bowl, and my servant tosses it. On the tossed salad I sprinkle a pinch of paprika, which is the Hungarian red pepper . . . And there you have the salad that so fascinated poor Ronconi.

– From Alexandre Dumas' *Dictionary of Cuisine*, edited, abridged and translated by Louis Colman

Sometime in 1844 or 1845, around the time that *The Three Musketeers* was published, French writer Alexandre Dumas was 'seized with remorse' that he was failing to keep up his custom of serving suppers, as he wrote in his *Le Grande Dictionnaire de Cuisine* of 1873. As a solution, he set up a table with fifteen places and offered standing invitations to friends among the writers, actors, publishers and playwrights of the day to stop by on Wednesdays between eleven p.m. and midnight for dinner. Those who couldn't make it would let him know three or four days in advance so he could fill their place. The menu for these meals was a pie made from game – hunted by Dumas himself – followed by a roast, fish and, as a *pièce de résistance*, a salad. The last was seasoned by the host's hand and assembled according to the most exacting seasonal principles.

At that time, Dumas was at a peak of his tumultuous career, and one of the most famous men in Paris. He was a tall, round-faced giant, described by biographers the Brothers de Goncourt as having 'clear and mischievous' eyes and 'puffing and blowing, and [being] in roistering good spirits'. His start in life had been somewhat dubious – he was the son of a mixed-race father and the grandson of a French marquis and an African slave from the French colony of Saint Domingue (now Haiti). He had no real family name – 'Dumas' was assumed by his father, and may have been from *du mas* (of the farm). But through a clever pen, savvy marketing and the cultivation of powerful men, Dumas achieved success first as a playwright, then as a novelist, with a few revolutions and setbacks in between.

Dumas's great love, however, was gastronomy. And in 1869, after having paid off a crushing fifteen-year debt, one of his many reversals of fortune, he retired to seaside Brittany. There he would compose a work he'd long dreamed of, which he referred to as 'the pillow of my old age', *Le Grand Dictionnaire de Cuisine.* The book is an eccentric, alphabetical compendium of the entirety of Dumas's research and wisdom on food and cooking, half recipe book and half social and historical commentary. Its introductory materials provide a history of dining customs and a celebration of great gastronomes, and display Dumas's inimitable discursive wit. Louis XVIII, he tells us, 'exhausted the mysteries of the most recherché luxury'. At his table 'ortolans stuffed with truffles were cooked in the stomachs of partridges'. Lawyer and politician Brillat-Savarin, author of *The Physiology of Taste*, on the other hand, was 'neither a gastronome nor a gourmet' and loved eating 'strong, vulgar foods'. In the introduction to the volume, Dumas writes: 'From birth man is instructed by his stomach to eat at least three times a day, to renew the strength he spends in labour, or as happens more often, in idleness. Eating is the great preoccupation of both primitive and civilized man. But the savage eats from need and the civilized man from desire.'

Le Grand Dictionnaire de Cuisine, naturally, is for the civilized man; Dumas's magnum opus also embraced conservative, traditional methods of food preparation. The book is currently not in print, but copies of an abridged and translated version published in the 1950s can be found online, and an essay by its editor and translator explains that Dumas's large test kitchen eschewed the modern technology of the time – like the gas range – in favour of traditional means of food preparation: by fireplace, grill, or baking oven heated with coals. The writer's fireplace had a spit in front with a dripping pan, 'notches set at appropriate distances from the fire', and was sometimes enhanced with a *four de campagne*, a term that could refer to one of two vintage cooking apparatuses. The first was an 'under and over' container, a braising pot with a special lid to be set in coals or hot ashes. The lid had a vertical stick for a handle (so you could lift it up to baste) and a raised lip that would allow you to pile coals above as well as below. (The heat would be similar to what's achieved now with a modern oven.) A different item by the same name was sometimes referred to in the colonial United States as a 'tin reflector oven', which was a sort of barrel-shaped, three-sided stove front that could be put in front of an open fireplace to keep the heat in. Lastly, Dumas had a giant mortar and pestle operated by rings and pulleys attached to the ceiling. It was an appropriate kitchen for a man who was larger-than-life.

Gerald Durrell

1925–95

A far-flung family table

Taj Mahal Tidbits

• Slices of toasted wheat bread • 8oz cheese, grated, paneer is best but Greek kasseri will do, feta also • 2 spring onions, chopped • 1 green chili finely chopped or grated • Pinch of cracked black pepper • 1 tbsp olive oil

Mix and mash the cheese, spring onions, chili and black pepper in a bowl and make a stiff paste with the olive oil. Then spread thickly on toast and brown under a grill till bubbling. Cut into fingers and serve.

– From *Dining with the Durrells* by David Shimwell

The origins of the Durrell family's move to Corfu in 1935 involved, legend has it, a cookbook. In *My Family and Other Animals*, animal conservationist and prolific memoirist-humorist Gerald Durrell detailed a family scene between his mother and his brother Larry – Lawrence Durrell, author of the *Alexandria Quartet*. Durrell's mother, Louisa, was born in India while under British rule and lived there for most of her life until moving to Bournemouth, England, with her four children after the death of their father Lawrence Samuel Durrell. Louisa was a prolific cook with a deep hereditary knowledge of regional Indian cooking, and remained connected to her culinary roots for all of her life. In Gerald's humorous recounting, she was so absorbed in reading a 'large volume entitled *Easy Recipes from Rajputana*' that when Larry suggested the family move to Corfu, she absentmindedly said yes. Larry was thrilled and 'Mother, perceiving that she had made a tactical error, cautiously lowered *Easy Recipes from Rajputana* . . .' Durrell writes.

The Durrells' life on Corfu became the subject of Gerald Durrell's best-known work, *The Corfu Trilogy*, as well as the inspiration for the television show *The Durrells* from 2016–19. The books primarily delight readers for their unequalled descriptions of the natural world, but throughout Durrell also turns the jewelled microscope of his attention to his family, including their dining rituals. The following passage gives some sense of his skill and signature humour:

> We ate breakfast out in the garden, under the small tangerine-trees. The sky was fresh and shining, not yet the fierce blue of noon, but a clear milky opal. The flowers were half-asleep, roses dew-crumpled, marigolds still tightly shut. Breakfast was, on the whole, a leisurely and silent meal, for no member of the family was talkative at that hour. By the end of the meal the influence of the coffee, toast and eggs made itself felt, and we started to revive, to tell each other what we intended to do, why we intended to do it, and then argue earnestly as to whether each had made a wise decision.

The Durrells ate some traditional English food, such as at breakfast, and they also followed the rituals of the English teatime, but Louisa's home cuisine was Indian, and even on Corfu she continued to make curries, chutneys and finger-foods like Madras Marvels or the Taj Mahal Tidbits mentioned above. She was the third generation of her family to be born in India while under British rule, and her recipe archive, which now resides at Les Augrès Manor in Jersey, includes family documents from as early as 1887. This unusual historical experience, combined with Gerald's literary representation of her cooking, inspired family friend David Shimwell to write the cookbook and history, *Dining with the Durrells*, published in 2019. Thus the specific family recipes are available for many of the dishes mentioned in *The Corfu Trilogy*. There's a recipe for the vegetable curry the family is forced to dine on after youthful naturalist Gerald has fed the pork chops intended

for their dinner to his baby owls. And there are also several recipes for cakes like Plum Cake (Indian) and Layer Cake that match Durrell's descriptions of 'Mother's gastronomic triumphs . . . cakes like snowdrifts, oozing jam; cakes dark, rich and moist crammed with fruit . . .'

In the cookbook's introduction, Gerald's widow Lee Durrell writes that the 'assembly, preparation and consumption of meals, from sumptuous feasts to simple fare, were a preoccupation of the Durrell family for over two generations'. Gerald carried on many of his mother's traditions after her death. He and Lee entertained frequently, especially at a farmhouse near Nîmes, France, that Lawrence Durrell sold to Gerald in 1982. They made taramasalata and skordalia from the family's Greek days, or 'cauldrons of chicken curry'. Lee recounts a special dish of Gerald's as 'the *pièce de resistance* – roasted quails encircling the lower elevations of a mountain of saffron rice, crowned by peeled quails' eggs, the summit dusted with paprika and parsley. Small potatoes and florets of cauliflower and broccoli were embedded in the side of the mountain and the whole was intermingled with sultanas, almonds and pine nuts, lightly bound with cream.' The dish, she writes, was worthy of Gerald's mother. And if some of the cookbooks Louisa consults in her son's work are humorous inventions – neither *Easy Recipes from Rajputana* nor another named book, *A Million Mouthwatering Oriental Recipes*, actually existed – mother and son's twinned legacies live on.

The Durrells ate some traditional English food, but Louisa's home cuisine was Indian, and even on Corfu she continued to make curries, chutneys and finger-foods like Taj Mahal Tidbits.

The Perfect Writer's Luncheon

Irving Stone's 10,000 Cheese Sandwiches

2 slices of white bread – dull, factory-baked, full-of-air, unadorned kind. 1 slice pasteurized American cheese – presliced too thin, to be sure no pimento mixed in, too exciting. Toast bread, lay cheese on one slice, cover with the other. On festive, daring occasions put open face in oven for a few minutes to get holiday change.

– From *The Artists' & Writers' Cookbook*, edited by Beryl Barr and Barbara Turner Sachs

'I have evolved the perfect writer's luncheon, and I have not deviated from it in thirty-five years,' wrote Irving Stone (1903–89) in *The Artists' & Writers' Cookbook*, published in 1961.

Stone, a California-born American, confessed that 'I am one of those writers who, as he gets halfway through a long book, decides that there is nothing he can possibly eat that will agree with him. I start out at page 1, line 1, weighing some 170 pounds, and a quarter of a million words later, in seventh draft and ready for the printer, I have come down to 145 pounds.'

Stone knew about long days and the routines of geniuses: he was the author of an acclaimed biographical novel about Michelangelo, *The Agony and the Ecstasy*, and one about Vincent Van Gogh, *Lust for Life*, in which he presented original research that the artist cut off his whole ear and not just the lobe. His solution to writing-related dyspepsia was a 'sole and complete lunch [consisting of] an American cheese sandwich on toast and a dish of tea'. The lunch was not delicious to him; in fact, its monotony was 'almost unbearable', but anything else – 'a tongue or beef sandwich, or even a piece of chicken' – gave him an upset stomach that prevented him from writing.

Stone wrote that, 'By a rough estimate, I think I have eaten ten thousand cheese sandwiches during my thirty-five years of concentrated writing. They reached their point of diminishing returns twenty-five years ago, but when one has to make a decision between dietary *ennui* or indigestion – what choice is there?'

F. Scott Fitzgerald

1896–1940

Drinking was the 'writer's vice'

Chicken Maryland

Cut a 3½ pound chicken into pieces. Dip each piece into milk, season with salt and pepper, dredge in flour, and let dry 30 minutes. In heavy skillet heat 3 tablespoons vegetable oil and sauté chicken on all sides until nicely browned. Add 1 cup hot water, ¼ teaspoon cumin, and ¼ teaspoon sage, and let come to boil. Immediately reduce heat, cover and let simmer 45 minutes. Remove lid and simmer until all moisture has evaporated from pan. Serve.

– From *Found Meals of the Lost Generation: Recipes and Anecdotes from 1920s Paris* by Suzanne Rodriguez-Hunter

'First you take a drink,' F. Scott Fitzgerald once noted, 'then the drink takes a drink, then the drink takes you.' The jazz-age icon also sometimes introduced himself as 'F. Scott Fitzgerald, the well-known alcoholic', and called drinking 'the writer's vice'. In these remarks he seems to flaunt his alcoholism, as he did continually jn letters to friends in the 1920s. To the literary critic Edmund Wilson, a friend from Princeton, he wrote in 1920, 'Since I last saw you I've tried to get married & then tried to drink myself to death but foiled, as have so many good men by the sex and the state, I have returned to literature.' A long letter to John Peale Bishop in 1929 found him boasting, 'excuse Christ-like tone of letter. Began tippling at page 2 and am now positively holy (like Dostoevsky's non-stinking monk).' Later, he grew ashamed, and his death in 1940 of complications related to alcoholism at age forty-four is a tragedy of American letters.

Nonetheless, Fitzgerald's snappy, humorous manner of speech on booze is notable as a testament to his view of the world. The writer understood that food and drink could express not just a person's social status, but their style and persona – what we might now call their personal brand. His brand was of American high society and jazz-age decadence, though personally he always felt a conflict between his glamorous life and his middle-class, Midwestern origins. Both he and his characters talked about eating and drinking to match the loose, cosmopolitan way they wished to be perceived. A buffet table is covered with 'glistening hors d'oeuvres' at Jay Gatsby's wild parties in Fitzgerald's third novel, *The Great Gatsby*. A 'journal' written by Fitzgerald and wife Zelda and published in *Esquire* in 1934 chronicles the couple's time drifting through Europe and staying in hotels in the 1920s, and consistently notes the food details: the gin fizzes at the Beau Monde in Paris, the 'strawberries in a gold dish' at Claridge's in London, and the *salade Niçoises* and 'very special bouillabaisse' on the French coastline near Nice.

In Fitzgerald's late masterpiece *Tender is the Night*, the characters Dick and Nicole Diver are an amalgam of Scott and Zelda and Gerald and

The writer understood that food and drink could express not just a person's social status, but their style and persona

Sara Murphy, the latter wealthy Americans living on the French Riviera with whom the Fitzgeralds were friendly in the 1920s. In the beginning of the novel, Dick and Nicole more closely resemble the confident, glamorous and influential Murphys – who were friends with Picasso and Gertrude Stein, and whose activities established much of the style and tenor of the times. (Sara Murphy's habit of tossing her string of pearls over her back while sunbathing on the beach has been immortalized in several paintings by Picasso, for an example of her cultural cachet.) Fitzgerald portrays Nicole in the novel's first scenes lounging on the beach, her 'ruddy, orange brown' back 'set off by a string of creamy pearls', while leafing through a cookbook contemplating what to serve for dinner. Her choice is 'Chicken Maryland'.

The recipe for this dish, above, was sourced from a 1994 cookbook, *Found Meals of the Lost Generation* by Suzanne Rodriguez-Hunter, and loosely based on a recipe from the 1930 edition of *The Joy of Cooking* by Irma S. Rombauer. The Chicken Maryland's appearance in *Tender is the Night* juxtaposes the familiar and domestic (choosing what to make for dinner) with the impossibly glamorous setting (French Rivieria, pearls), and displays the yearning throughout Fitzgerald's work to live not just a life but a *lifestyle*. And in all his novels, the yearning after this fleeting, champagne-bubble ideal goes badly. Dick and Nicole Diver quickly become the dysfunctional Scott and Zelda Fitzgerald, lives riddled by alcohol abuse, suicide and madness.

Fitzgerald died in 1940, believing himself a failure and his work forgotten, but his beautiful stylings, so emblematic of the jazz age, live on.

Johann Wolfgang von Goethe

1749–1832

The It-boy of the 1700s

I crossed the courtyard to a well-built house and, climbing the flight of steps in front, opened the door and beheld the most charming scene I have ever set eyes on. In the hallway, six children aged between eleven and two were milling about a girl with a wonderful figure and of medium height, wearing a simple white dress with pink ribbons at the sleeves and breast. She was holding a loaf of rye bread and cutting a piece for each of the little ones about her, according to their age and appetite; she handed out the slices with great kindliness, and the children reached up their little hands long before the bread was cut . . .

– From *The Sorrows of Young Werther* by Johann Wolfgang von Goethe

The eighteenth-century poet, playwright, novelist, scientist and statesman, Johann Wolfgang von Goethe, one of the founders of the *Sturm und Drang* movement in German literature, tended his asparagus patch even as a wild youth, and sent the woman he loved baskets of vegetables. 'One's home is half one's life,' he wrote in a letter in 1795. Throughout his work and life he showed an appreciation for simple and domestic pleasures, as in the passage above.

The Young Goethe was a preternaturally brilliant boy from a burgher family in Frankfurt, who was tutored at home by his father, learned to draw and play the harpsichord, and had a great facility for languages. In 1774, while pursuing a desultory career in law, the twenty-five-year-old wrote *The Sorrows of Young Werther*, a partially tongue-in-cheek, autobiographical novel-in-letters on a young man's love for a woman betrothed to another that became an international sensation. *Sturm und Drang* insisted on the value of inner and emotional states, and on the importance of representing them in works of art. Goethe's tale of Werther's doomed love did this so well it went viral, eighteenth-century style. 'Perhaps there never was a fiction which so startled and enraptured the world,' Goethe biographer George Henry Lewes wrote in 1855. 'Men of all kinds and classes were moved by it. It was the companion of Napoleon when in Egypt: it penetrated in to China.'

Following the success of *The Sorrows of Young Werther*, Goethe left his native Frankfurt to join the entourage of the young Karl August, Duke of Saxe, in Weimar in 1775, where he was the centre of a group of rowdy young men who drank to excess and did crazy-for-the-time stunts like shaving their heads while in their cups (intoxicated) and sleeping in peasant huts. In the introduction to an 1885 collection of the writer's early letters, editor Edward Bell writes that Goethe and the gang 'visited all the great houses of the neighbourhood, sometimes starting for the day's expedition at early morning, and taking with them their own wines and provisions in a sumpter-wagon'.

Nonetheless, Goethe took his responsibilities to society seriously. In joining the duke, he gave up his writing time for a role in government. 'Amidst all the temptations of luxury in living, Goethe never allowed himself to fall into habits of self-indulgence,' Bell writes. He was fond of the light German wines, objected to tea and coffee, rose early, loved to bathe in cold water and would sometimes sleep outside on a stone bench wrapped in a cloak. For the duke, he advised on highway construction, mining and reform of the universities.

Two of Goethe's former homes in Weimar have become house museums. One is the garden cottage where he lived upon first joining the duke in 1775. The writer himself oversaw renovations to its grounds. He instructed workers to terrace the land, put in stairs and pathways, and plant flowers and trees. On the lower grounds he planted a vegetable garden, which grew strawberries and potatoes. It was during this period that he met and fell in love with Charlotte von Stein, an older, married woman, with whom he carried on a correspondence and possibly an affair for ten years. Biographer Rüdiger Safranski in *Goethe: Life as a Work of Art* mentions Goethe staying at home to tend his asparagus patch while in a spat with von Stein, and sending her his garden vegetables during the good times.

When Goethe committed himself to the duke, he did so for life. In 1782 he moved to a stately home on Frauenplan square in Weimar and lived there for almost fifty years. Here too he took personal interest in all aspects of the house, including its garden, which supplied the household with fruit and vegetables, and was planted with asparagus, artichokes, apricots and grapes. His financial records from this time have been preserved – an enormous 20,000 of them – and they show him eating very well. Scholar W. Daniel Wilson, professor emeritus of German at Royal Holloway, University of London, who spent substantial time in the archives, regularly found invoices for items like caviar and Malaga wine. 'It seemed often to be the case that as the morning in the archive wore on and my stomach was growling, I came across things like invoices for a chicken fricassee from the restaurant across the street or something similar,' he says. 'Something of a torture.'

Ernest Hemingway

1899–1961

Nature was his movable feast

Fried Trout

• 1 cup Crisco or vegetable shortening • 4 whole trout, cleaned • 1 cup of cornmeal • 8 slices of bacon

The proper way to cook is over coals. Have several cans of Crisco or Cotosuet or one of the vegetable shortenings along that are as good as lard. Put the bacon in and when it is about half cooked lay the trout in the hot grease, dipping them in cornmeal first. Then put the bacon on top of the trout and it will baste them as it slowly cooks . . .

– From Ernest Hemingway, the *Toronto Star* (as reproduced in *The Hemingway Cookbook* by Craig Boreth)

'Papa' Hemingway, as Ernest was called in his middle age, learned from *his* papa how to make the most of nature's bounty, in terms of hunting, fishing, trapping and cooking in the wild. Hemingway has gone down in history as 'a ruggedly physical man of action', according to biographer Mary V. Dearborn. His passion for adventure started young, learned from his father Dr Clarence 'Ed' Hemingway, an eccentric Illinois doctor who embodied the spirit of the American frontier.

Dr Hemingway made his own bullets in the family's basement, pulled taffy for candy and taught his eldest son the ways of the wild, including 'how to walk like an Indian, how to preserve and stuff animals after they were dead, [and] how to tie flies to catch trout', Dearborn wrote. He was known for being able to cook whatever he'd shot, trapped or gathered. A paean to food in Hemingway's life, published in 1994 by the *San Diego Reader*, reveals Hemingway's papa as making gooseberry pie and peach turnovers, canning fruits and vegetables, and having an elaborate Christmas routine. Hemingway senior would cure beef in the fruit cellar, bake mince pies, and set boiled, spiced pork hocks in bowls in the back yard to cure and freeze. 'On Christmas Eve, Dr. Hemingway would open his preserved fruits and vegetables, serve hockies, pickles, mince pies and cut the oven-roasted beef so thin the slices curled,' the paper writes, culling the details from the book *Along with Youth: Hemingway, The Early Years* by Peter Griffin.

Hemingway became a connoisseur of oysters during the Paris years

When Hemingway moved to Paris with his first wife, Hadley Richardson, he encountered a new kind of dining, which he took to with gusto. He learned to choose wines and appreciated fine-dining menus, such as one with 'roast beef, veal cutlet, lamb mutton, thick steaks, all served with the most delicious potatoes he'd ever tasted, and brussels sprouts in butter, creamed spinach, peas, and salad . . .' the *San Diego Reader* says. And he observed the niceties of the table. 'At Ernest's insistence, Hadley would make a ceremony of preparing salad dressing at their table.'

Hemingway also became a connoisseur of oysters during the Paris years. In *The Hemingway Cookbook*, Craig Boreth says that the author enjoyed 'the superior quality marennes, or cultivated oysters . . . which are large and bright green in color. In the 1920s they were considered very expensive at $1.50 a dozen.' Hemingway's autobiography *A Moveable Feast*, which he wrote in the late 1950s, mined a cache of his papers from his early days in Paris, and records his experience of the oysters as the following: 'As I ate the oysters with their strong taste of the sea and their faint metallic taste that the cold white wine washed away, leaving only the sea taste and the succulent texture, and as I drank their cold liquid from each shell and washed it down with the crisp taste of the wine, I lost the empty feeling and began to be happy and to make plans.'

A precise eye for detail and a rigorous observation of simple routine may have been Hemingway's means of blotting out the trauma of his experiences during the First World War, Dearborn writes. It was also, of course, a way to blaze a totally new literary style. In the story *Big Two-Hearted River*, a stand-in for the author heals himself with campfire cooking and shows the technique:

> Nick was hungry. He did not believe he had ever been hungrier. He opened and emptied a can of pork and beans and a can of spaghetti into the frying pan …
>
> Nick put the frying pan on the grill over the flames. He was hungrier. The beans and spaghetti warmed. Nick stirred them and mixed them together. They began to bubble, making little bubbles that rose with difficulty to the surface. There was a good smell. Nick got out a bottle of tomato catchup and cut four slices of bread. The little bubbles were coming faster now. Nick sat down beside the fire and lifted the frying pan off. He poured about half the contents out into the tin plate. It spread slowly on the plate. Nick knew it was too hot. He poured on some tomato catchup … Across the river in the swamp, in the almost dark, he saw a mist rising. He looked at the tent once more. All right. He took a full spoonful from the plate. 'Chrise,' Nick said, 'Geezus Chrise.'

Zora Neale Hurston

1891–1960

'I've been in sorrow's kitchen and licked out all the pots'

Tea Cakes

Makes 24

• 60g (2oz/¼ cup) unsalted butter, at room temperature • 60g (2oz/¼ cup) vegetable shortening • 200g (7oz/1 cup) sugar • 1 egg, at room temperature • Grated zest of 1 lemon • Seeds scraped from ½ vanilla bean • 260g (9¼oz/2 cups) plain (all-purpose) flour, plus extra for dusting • 2 tsp baking powder • ½ tsp salt • ⅛ tsp nutmeg • 60ml (2fl oz/¼ cup) buttermilk

In an electric mixer, cream together the butter and shortening. Add the sugar and mix until light and fluffy. Mix in the egg, lemon zest and vanilla seeds. Set aside.

In a medium bowl, sift together the flour, baking powder, salt and nutmeg. Mix the dry ingredients into the wet ingredients, alternating with the buttermilk.

Turn the dough out onto a lightly floured surface and knead until smooth. Shape into a disc and cover with cling film (plastic wrap). Chill for 1 hour. Towards the end of the chilling time, preheat the oven to 180°C/350°F/gas 4.

Remove the dough from the refrigerator and roll it out to a sheet about 5mm (¼in) thick, using extra flour to prevent it from sticking. Use a 7.5cm (3in) round cookie cutter (or a drinking glass with similar dimensions) to cut out circles. Place the tea cakes on a baking sheet, spacing them about 2.5cm (1in) apart. Bake for 8–10 minutes until bottoms are golden.

– Adapted from a recipe by Valerie Stivers for *The Paris Review*

Throughout *Their Eyes Were Watching God*, the 1937 novel on Black Southern womanhood by Zora Neale Hurston, people eat soda crackers with cheese, drink lemonade or sweeten their water with ribbon cane syrup, and serve whole barbecued hogs with sweet-potato pone (a Caribbean side dish or dessert). A man on a spree offers fried chicken and macaroni for all, and Janie, the heroine, leaves her first husband after frying him a hoe-cake to go with his coffee. 'She dumped the dough on the skillet and smoothed it over with her hand. She wasn't even angry,' Hurston writes.

Instead of a loveless marriage, Janie insists on having the sweet things in life. Her second husband buys her 'the best things the butcher had, like apples and a glass lantern full of candies'. And her great love is a handsome man fifteen years her junior whom everyone calls 'Tea Cake'. (A tea cake is a classic of Southern cooking that's actually a simple round of sugar dough with a crisp bottom and chewy texture, something between a scone and a cookie.) Hurston's belief that the pursuit of happiness and sensuality was a worthy life goal, especially for a Black woman, was radical when the book was published, and she was criticized for being 'pseudo-primitive', too female, too personal, not promoting Black causes in the right way. She died in obscurity in 1960.

Hurston was rediscovered in the 1970s thanks to the efforts of *The Color Purple* author Alice Walker. In the years since, her portrayals of the rich, tumultuous Black American life of her time have become canonical. Her part in that life started in Alabama in 1891, in a family where all four of the grandparents had been born in slavery. Her parents moved to the all-Black town of Eatonville, Florida, when Hurston was three years old, where her father became the mayor. They lived in a large home on a self-sufficient homestead with five acres of land that grew oranges, tangerines, grapefruits, spring greens (or collards), and raised hogs and chickens. The Hurstons didn't have running water, and the author recalled her mother washing the greens in a stream, and making preserves from the farm's guavas, pears and peaches. 'We had all the eggs we wanted,' Hurston once said, according to the book *Zora Neale Hurston on Florida Food* by Fred Opie, which draws on Hurston's non-fiction and ethnographic writings. And it was 'a common thing for us smaller children to fill the iron tea kettle full of eggs and boil them and lay around in the yard and eat them until we were full. Any leftover boiled eggs could always be used for missiles.'

Hurston was given a scholarship to Barnard College in 1925, where she was the only Black person in her class. She studied anthropology under Franz Boas, and devoted much of the rest of her life to recording the oral histories and traditions of Black Americans. In her private life, she liked to garden. Her favourite things to cook were shrimp and okra, and when she was low on money she made cornbread and served it with buttermilk. Opie quotes her in a letter from May 1936, writing, 'My work is coming on most satisfactorily and I feel fine. I get up before sunrise and work on a tiny garden.' She was growing black-eyed peas, pole beans and lima beans, and in a later letter from the same summer, mentions that her garden is in 'full swing' and that she has so many peas she plans to send a hamper of them into town to be sold.

Hurston's indomitable spirit and zest for life is perhaps best captured by a quotation from a rare oral recording, in which she says, 'I've been in sorrow's kitchen and licked out all the pots.' Audrey Sprenger, a visiting professor of sociology and the humanities at two Florida universities, believes that sensuality is one of the keys to Hurston. She offers students in her introductory humanities courses bonus points for baking tea cakes (recipe above) during the module on *Their Eyes Were Watching God*. 'The purpose is to provide students a sensory experience to better connect them to the author and book,' she says.

Her favourite things to cook were shrimp and okra, and when she was low on money she made cornbread and served it with buttermilk.

Franz Kafka

1883–1924

He hated his body

Hard Pretzels with Caraway Seeds

Makes 24
• 400g (14oz/3 cups) plain (all-purpose) flour • 2 tsp brown sugar • ½ tsp salt • 1¼ tsp yeast, proofed • 180ml (6fl oz/¾ cup) warm water • Oil, for greasing • 2 tbsp food-grade lye (sodium hydroxide) • 2 tbsp coarse sea salt • 1 tbsp caraway seeds • Vinegar or lemon juice to hand (to neutralize possible lye burns)

Put the yeast in a small bowl and add 60ml (2fl oz/¼ cup) of the warm water and a pinch of the sugar. Stir together then leave for a few minutes to activate the yeast.

In the bowl of a stand mixer, combine the flour, sugar and salt. Add the yeast and the remaining warm water and knead with a dough hook, for 5 minutes until smooth and elastic. Transfer to a lightly oiled bowl and set aside to rise until roughly doubled in size.

Next, prepare a lye bath with the lye and 1 litre (35fl oz/4 cups) water – use a number 2 or number 5 plastic container and a silicone spatula to stir, taking all safety precautions. Lye is a caustic substance so must be handled very carefully.

Preheat your oven to 170°C/325°F/gas 3. Set out a small bowl of water, and two baking sheets lined with oiled baking parchment.

Combine the coarse sea salt with the caraway seeds and set aside for topping.

When the dough has risen, cut it in quarters. Roll each quarter into a log, then cut the log into fifths. Cover all the dough with a damp towel. Working with one piece of dough at a time, use your hands to roll the piece into a 38–46cm (15–18in) strand. Make a ‘U’ shape with the dough, then cross the arms to make a pretzel shape. Dab the underside of the arms with water to make them stick. Repeat with all the dough, placing them on the prepared baking sheets as you go. Cover, and let them rise for an additional 10 minutes. Using a slotted spatula, dip each pretzel into the lye bath for approximately 30 seconds, then return to the baking sheet.

When all pretzels are dipped, sprinkle them with the topping. Bake for 25 minutes, then rotate the pans and switch them round on the shelves and bake for a further 40 minutes until crisp and dark brown. (The steam created during baking will neutralize the lye and make the pretzels safe to handle and eat.)

– Adapted from a recipe by Valerie Stivers for *The Paris Review*

Franz Kafka's first published story, 'Description of a Struggle', depicts the narrator sitting in a drawing room at a rickety little table, eating a piece of fruitcake that 'did not taste very good', when a man walks up to him. The man is described as an 'acquaintance', but is actually a double, or another part of the narrator's self. The acquaintance has fallen in love and wants to boast about it. 'If you weren't in such a state,' the narrator scolds him, '[you] would know how improper it is to talk about an amorous girl to a man sitting alone drinking schnapps.' The comment seems to threaten an unchecked appetite. What would the lonely, schnapps-drinking man do if tempted by the girl? The struggle that follows, metaphorically speaking, is between the two sides of the protagonist's character – the man who desires to stand apart from society and guard his creative self, and he who wishes to fit in and reap the pleasures of fruitcake and amorous girls.

The tension in Kafka between appetite and its fulfilment is a crucial aspect of the writer's work. Kafka's characters are often hungry – the performer from the short story 'A Hunger Artist' has made starving himself into an art; Gregor Samsa from the novella *The Metamorphosis* slowly stops eating and wastes away. But their hunger is often not for the foods of this world. Gregor refers to himself as hungering for 'an unknown nourishment'. The hunger artist's last words are a confession that fasting was not difficult for him because, he says, 'I couldn't find the food I liked. If I had found it, believe me, I should have made no fuss and stuffed myself like you or anyone else.' Instead, the characters seek the deeper forms of sustenance – emotional, societal, sexual, spiritual – but don't usually find them.

Franz Kafka's characters often expressed his own psychological state. Scholars widely agree that Kafka had what is now considered to be anorexia. He ate a vegetarian diet, was always extremely thin, and believed that fasting helped him to write. On 3 January 1912 he wrote in his diary, as quoted in a story on Kafka's eating disorder by Rachel Veroff for HuffPost: 'I dieted in all these directions' (meaning, abstaining from alcohol, sex and food). 'When it became clear that writing was the most productive direction for my being to take, everything rushed in that direction, and left empty all other of my abilities.' Veroff also quotes that he once wrote in a letter to his second fiancée, Milena Jesenská, 'No one sings as purely as those who inhabit the deepest hell ... I am dirty, Milena, infinitely dirty, this is why I scream so much about purity.' Kafka died of tuberculosis in 1924 at the age of forty, and his writing only survives because his friend Max Brod disobeyed his orders to burn all of it. The salt- and caraway-seed-encrusted hard pretzel recipe above is a classic German and Bohemian treat – Kafka was a German-language writer from Prague – mentioned in his last unfinished novel, *The Castle*. They are crunched on by an official and symbolize the rewards of power. The character K, the writer's stand-in, does not taste them, of course.

The tension in Kafka between appetite and its fulfillment is a crucial aspect of the writer's work.

Han Kang

1970–present

Renunciation as a moral good

If you'd said my wife had always been faintly nauseated by meat, then I could have understood it, but in reality it was quite the opposite – ever since we'd got married she had proved herself a more than competent cook, and I'd always been impressed by her way with food. Tongs in one hand and a large pair of scissors in the other, she'd flipped rib meat in a sizzling pan while snipping it into bite-sized pieces, her movements deft and practiced. Her fragrant, caramelized deep-fried pork belly was achieved by marinading the meat in minced ginger and glutinous starch syrup. Her signature dish had been wafer-thin slices of beef seasoned with black pepper and sesame oil, then coated with sticky rice powder as generously as you would with rice cakes or pancakes, and dipped in bubbling shabu-shabu broth.

– From *The Vegetarian* by Han Kang

Han Kang, the winner of the 2024 Nobel Prize in Literature, was the first Korean winner, the first Asian woman to win, and, at fifty-three years old, the fifth-youngest winner ever. The Prize was awarded to her for 'her intense poetic prose that confronts historical traumas and exposes the fragility of human life', according to the organization's website. Or, as writer Yung In Chae put it on the website of *The Yale Review*, 'with little more than paper and ink, [Han Kang] acts as a conduit for the memories of generations that suffered state violence, passing them on to generations that inherited these traumas but not necessarily the long-suppressed facts beneath them'. Post-Nobel Prize, the writer's novels quickly sold more than a million copies locally, a landmark in Korean publishing.

Han Kang's 2007 novel, *The Vegetarian*, won the Man Booker International Prize in 2016 when it was published in translation, and remains one of her best-selling and most accessible works. The novel tells the story of Yeong-hye, a seemingly ordinary married woman who gives up eating meat after an appalling and bloody dream about people enjoying a barbecue. She is seen at first through the eyes of her angry, abusive husband, and then, in the book's third section, through the eyes of her brother-in-law, who becomes sexually obsessed with her.

Kang's central preoccupation is with how human beings treat each other. 'I wanted to ask what it is that makes human beings harm others so brutally, and how we ought to understand those who never lose hold of their humanity in the face of violence. I wanted to grope toward a bridge spanning the yawning chasm between savagery and dignity,' she explained in an interview published by the Booker Prize Committee.

The vegetarian woman's act of renouncing meat is symbolically a rejection of harming others. By the standards of the people around her, the woman is crazy, but she finds a kind of bliss through her freedom from human appetite. For her, the affair with her brother-in-law seems to represent an escape from the bonds of human society, and perhaps even an escape from being human. By the end of the book the woman has stopped eating entirely and is trying to turn into a tree or a plant. Perhaps human beings are so inherently bad, the novel suggests, that the only ethical act is not to be one.

Han Kang in person is soft-spoken, shrinks from publicity, and also seems inclined to renounce eating and drinking on ethical grounds. Following her Nobel Prize win, when asked during the formal post-award call from the Swedish Academy how she was going to celebrate, she answered, 'After this phone call I'd like to have tea – I don't drink – I'm going to have tea with my son and I'll celebrate it quietly tonight.' She also reportedly told her father, the writer Han Seung-won, that he should 'refrain from hosting a celebratory banquet for her because of the two wars raging in Ukraine and Palestine', according to Yung In Chae in *The Yale Review*.

It's noteworthy then how well Han Kang writes about food when she wants to. The description quoted above from *The Vegetarian* is one of the novel's many detailed and appetizing descriptions of Korean food. One of the book's best set-pieces takes place during an important business dinner for Yeong-hye's husband at a Korean–Chinese restaurant, where her refusal to eat meat embarrasses her husband and horrifies his colleagues. Nonetheless, the following dishes sound delicious: 'mung bean jelly, dressed with thin slivers of green-pea jelly, mushrooms and beef'; 'fried chicken in a chili and garlic sauce'; and 'sticky-rice porridge . . . [using] a special recipe involving beef stock to give it a rich, luxurious taste'. And even the simple fare Yeong-hye *will* eat has its appeal: salad, kimchi, squash porridge, a slice of apple and a single orange segment, lettuce, soybean paste, plain seaweed soup.

In the third section of *The Vegetarian*, Yeong-hye's conventional and sceptical sister imagines her saying, '*Look, sister, I'm doing a handstand; leaves are growing out of my body, roots are sprouting out of my hands . . . they delve down into the earth. Endlessly, endlessly . . . yes, I spread my legs because I wanted flowers to bloom from my crotch . . .*'. Reluctantly, the sister sees the beauty of non-harmfulness, and of being a vegetarian.

Jack Kerouac

1922–69

The Beat who loved his mom's cooking

Ham and Split Pea Soup

Serves 4

• 1 tbsp butter • 2 tbsp olive oil • 1 white onion, chopped • 1 garlic clove, minced • 270g (9½oz/1½ cups) dried split peas • 1 meaty ham bone or smoked ham hock • 1 tsp onion powder • 1 bay leaf • leaves from 2 sprigs of thyme • 1.5 litres (52fl oz/6 cups) chicken stock, plus extra if needed to loosen • 200g (7oz/1½ cups) potatoes, cubed • 175g (6oz/1½ cups) carrots, chopped • Salt and black pepper

Heat the butter and olive oil in a saucepan on medium-high heat, add the onion and sauté until translucent, stirring frequently. Add the garlic and sauté until fragrant, then add the dried split peas, ham bone or ham hock, onion powder, bay leaf, thyme leaves and chicken stock. Cover and bring to a simmer. Let the soup simmer for 30 minutes, then add the potatoes and carrots and cook for another 20 minutes until the vegetables are tender. Remove the ham bone or hock and the bay leaves. Pull roughly 280g (10oz/2 cups) of meat off the bone, chop it into smaller pieces and return to the soup. If the soup is too thick, add an extra splash of water or stock. Season with salt and pepper, and serve.

– Adapted from a recipe by Valerie Stivers for *The Paris Review*

Jack Kerouac's *On the Road* is such an iconic American novel – an exemplar of the Beat literary style as well as of the road-trip genre – that it's surprising but also quintessentially American that it was written by a child of French-Canadian immigrants who became a cultural outsider. Jack Kerouac grew up in an insular Franco-American family in Lowell, Massachusetts, tied firmly to his mother by the tragedy of an older brother's death. He stayed home from school a lot, ate his mom's home-cooking, spoke mostly French until his teens, and all the while he read books 'in that blind indiscriminate way of book hungry children', according to writer Joyce Johnson in *The Voice is All: The Lonely Victory of Jack Kerouac*. Johnson met Kerouac in 1957 when she was twenty-one, nine months before the publication of *On the Road.* He lived with her on and off during the next two years. Johnson has written seven books, including the memoir, *Minor Characters*, on her life with the Beats.

Once Kerouac left home the rest was history. After a few years on a football scholarship to Columbia University, he dropped out to write full time, experience life, do a lot of drinking and partying, and, famously, to hit the road. The lust for life expressed by the Beats demanded playfulness and indulgence of all their appetites: for sex, freedom, parties, dancing, self-expression and food and drink. In *On the Road,* Sal Paradise, the Kerouac stand-in, follows Dean Moriarty (the character based on real-life Beat icon Neal Cassady) heading west. He explains, 'all my New York friends were in the negative, nightmare position of putting down society . . . but Dean just raced in society, eager for bread and love; he didn't care one way or the other . . . "so long's we can *eat*, son, y'car me? I'm *hungry*, I'm *starving*, let's *eat right now!*"' When Dean arrives in New York, he and his 'beautiful little sharp chick Marylou' head to a cafeteria to spend money on 'beautiful big glazed cakes and creampuffs'. Sal, on the road, seems to be always eating 'mountainous' scoops of ice cream and slices of pie, such as 'the sweetest cherry pie in Nebraska'.

Joyce Johnson, however, remembers a more rooted side to Kerouac, who loved when she cooked for him. 'I wasn't much of a cook at the time,' Johnson says – her mother deliberately hadn't taught her – however Kerouac 'was extremely grateful' and praised her simple cooking. One of his favourite dishes was pea soup, a speciality of his mother's. Audrey Sprenger, a sociology professor at the New College of Florida who specializes in Kerouac, explains that 'when he wrote his stream-of-consciousness novels he went into work-out mode, doing headstands every morning and a lot of running. He would subsist on pea soup because he thought it was nourishing.' Johnson cooked only the instant Lipton variety, sometimes adding bacon, and she made other simple foods, like eggs with apple sauce on the side, or hamburgers with tinned or frozen peas. But they made the writer happy.

Johnson also fondly remembers ordering the cheapest item on the menu at an Italian restaurant in New York's Greenwich Village that Kerouac and his friends frequented. The restaurant was referred to as 'the Baci place', and the dish was pasta with pesto, for sixty cents. And once, on a weekend at a farmhouse in New York State owned by fellow Beat Lucien Carr, inspired by the windfall apples on the ground, she made her first ever apple pie, following the recipe on a packet of Graham crackers for the crust. Kerouac liked it so much he called it 'an ecstasy pie', Johnson says, and he and Carr danced around and sprayed Reddi-wip (whipped cream) on it.

Kerouac's tragedy was alcoholism, and he died in 1969 at age forty-seven of an abdominal haemorrhage related to the disease. As an adult, he shared a house with his parents in Ozone Park, Queens, and then a series of houses with his mother after his father's death. In *The Voice is All*, Johnson writes that during this era '[h]is existence . . . was celibate, lonely, and largely devoted to his work', punctuated by massive binge weekends in the city. In later life Kerouac felt a painful duality between his two worlds, according to Johnson. But hopefully he still managed to enjoy his mother's cooking.

D.H. Lawrence

1885–1930

He baked an apology cake

Summer Cake with Any Fruit

Serves 10

For the batter:

• 115g (4oz/1 stick) unsalted butter, softened, plus extra for greasing • 100g (3½oz/½ cup) sugar • 130g (4½oz/1 cup) plain (all-purpose) flour • 1 tsp bicarbonate of soda (baking soda) • A pinch of salt • 2 eggs, at room temperature

For the topping:

• 680g (1lb 8oz/4 cups) soft summer fruit or berries, chopped • ½ tsp ground cinnamon • ¼ tsp ground ginger • 50g (1¾oz/¼ cup) white sugar • 50g (1¾oz/¼ cup) brown sugar • Juice of ½ lemon

Preheat the oven to 180°C/350°F/gas 4. Butter a 20cm (8in) springform cake pan. Line the bottom with baking parchment and butter the parchment.

To make the batter, cream together the butter and sugar in a stand mixer. In a separate small bowl, stir together the flour, bicarbonate of soda and salt. Add the eggs to the mixer one at a time, alternating with the flour mixture and mixing between additions.

To make the topping, combine all the ingredients in a mixing bowl, and toss to combine.

Spread the batter evenly into the pan and top with the fruit mixture. Place the tin on a foil-lined baking sheet to catch any juices and bake for 45–50 minutes. When the cake is done, a tester inserted into the centre will come out clean of batter, though streaked with fruit juices. Serve warm.

– Adapted from a recipe by Valerie Stivers for *The Paris Review*

David Herbert Lawrence lived precariously and ate hand-to-mouth for all of his short life, yet somehow still tasted the world's treasures. The writer was born into poverty in the English Midlands where his most enduring work, *Lady Chatterley's Lover*, takes place. He was the son of a coal miner and an educated woman come down in the world. His third novel, *Sons and Lovers*, written in his early twenties, was briefly fashionable in London for its realistic portrayal of the lower classes. But quickly the trouble began. Lawerence's work was thoguht too sexual, too grossly physical – as if it were written 'with one hand in the slime', said one of his detractors. From that point on, his writing was censored and suppressed. He and the love of his life, Frieda von Richthofen, were often forced abroad, where they could live cheaply while the authorities were looking for Lawrence in England.

Lawrence's views on sexuality and gender were controversial for his time – and still are today. He believed in essential male and female life-forces, and in his writing he treated the sexual union of a man and a woman as the foundational structure of human life. But he wasn't macho, and in many ways he played against type. Lawrence believed that shyness and softness were manly qualities. He did all the cooking and cleaning for himself and Frieda, and was known for making good bread. They took refuge in the United States for several months in 1924 and 1925 when a wealthy friend offered them the use of a cabin eighteen miles north of Taos. There, Lawrence ran the household, according to the biography, *D.H. Lawrence: The Life of an Outsider*, by John Worthen. The cabin, called the Kiowa Ranch, had no electricity, but the writer kept chickens, built an outdoor oven, made 'a meat safe to hang from a tree branch,' and travelled two miles on horseback for his milk and mail, butter and eggs.

Lawrence doesn't often refer to food in his letters, 'because it was such a normal part of everyday life that he never boasted about it', Worthen says. But he was a good cook, and his interest is apparent in some of his travel writing, particularly the three books he wrote about his trips to Italy,

He did all the cooking and cleaning for himself and Frieda, and was known for making good bread.

Twilight in Italy, *Sea and Sardinia* and *Sketches of Etruscan Places*. (Lawrence wrote such works for money when he couldn't get his fiction published.) In these books, collected as the Penguin Classics edition *D.H. Lawrence and Italy*, he often notes what he's served at the inn or by his hosts. For example, 'soup and boiled beef and vegetables' or 'a piece of cheese weighing about five pounds, and large fresh sweet cakes for breakfast'. In the latter case, he notes, 'I ate and was thankful: the food was good.' When it's not good, he's irritated. In one instance he chooses wine over beer because he suspects the inn's beer won't be cold enough.

Lawrence had a tempestuous relationship with Frieda, but was always trying to rope friends into communal living. After one spectacular domestic quarrel, he baked a cake by way of apology to the couple's friends, who were witnesses. The recipe above is a speculation of what such a cake might have been like, using simple ingredients that Lawrence would have had access to in New Mexico or elsewhere on his travels.

The Swiss Chalet

2201 WILSHIRE BLVD.
SANTA MONICA, CAL.

Thomas Mann

1875–1955

Schniztel and ice cream in Los Angeles

Since they had all eaten lunch earlier than usual today, they consumed large amounts of cookies and tea. But no sooner had they finished than a large crystal bowl filled with a yellow, grainy puree was passed around: almond crème, a mixture of eggs, ground almonds, and rosewater. It tasted quite wonderful, but one spoonful too much and you ended up with the most awful stomach ache. Nevertheless, even though Madame Buddenbrook begged them 'to leave a little corner for dinner,' they helped themselves freely. And Klothilde performed miracles. In grateful silence, she spooned up almond crème as if it were porridge. And now came little glasses of sabayon to refresh their palates – served with English plum cake …

– From *Buddenbrooks* by Thomas Mann

Because Thomas Mann's first great novel *Buddenbrooks* was historical, set between 1835 and 1877 and concerning the decline of a family of the German Hanseatic ruling elite, the writer is often associated more with the nineteenth century than the twentieth. Thus it's quite a shock to find him living in a modernist house in Los Angeles in the 1950s, surrounded by lemon and palm trees. Mann, a member of the Hanseaten himself, published *Buddenbrooks* in 1901 when he was only twenty-five, and as the passage quoted above indicates, he already saw clearly the decadence and folly of his cultural heritage, which he often expressed through food metaphors. His masterpiece, *The Magic Mountain*, contains many scenes of grotesque feasting as well. Later, Mann was also an early outspoken voice condemning Hitler: The author's activities as an opponent of the Nazi regime in the 1930s landed him and his large family in exile, eventually in America, first at Princeton, and then in Los Angeles.

Mann's devotion to his writing routine was legendary and his diaries are some of the most exhaustive in literary posterity. He was also a smoker, with a nervous stomach and ascetic habits, who remained 'whippet thin' throughout his life, according to Princeton professor emeritus Stanley Corngold, writing in *The Mind in Exile*, a book about Mann's time at Princeton. But he took an active part in world affairs, was a fixture on the German expatriate scene in Los Angeles, and enjoyed life in general, at least sometimes. 'Mann, let it be known, had a very lively relation to good food and drink,' Corngold writes. 'In his diaries, the patrician can suddenly seem very human, *un homme* (even a bit more than) *moyen sensual.*'

Mann dined at the White House with his hero, Franklin Delano Roosevelt, who he believed was 'a messianic counterfigure to the barbarian leader in his homeland', according to Nikolai Blaumer, co-editor with Benno Herz of *Thomas Mann's Los Angeles: Stories From Exile 1940–1952*. He was dazzled, but he wrote afterwards that the food was bad. Blaumer and Herz's book is a tribute to all the places Mann loved and the people he knew in Los Angeles, where the house that he built at 1550 North San Remo Drive has become a location for artist residencies. 'Time and again, people come to the Thomas Mann House and tell us stories about Thomas Mann, his family, and the exile community in Los Angeles,' the book begins. 'They tell us where someone met Mann for schnitzel or ice cream, where they would think about the political dilemmas of the day.' Another anecdote has Mann refreshing himself with 'beer, meatloaf and eggs' on 1 April 1938, after an address to 6,000 people at LA's Shrine Auditorium on fighting Fascism and 'The Coming Victory of Democracy', and staying up until 2a.m.

Two restaurants in particular were important to Mann during his time in LA. His regular lunch spot was the restaurant at the Fairmont Miramar Hotel, which exists to this day as a luminous landscape of globe lighting and sinuous blue-velvet banquettes. After his regular morning of writing and his constitutional walk along the Pacific Palisades, he also often lunched at Max's Swiss Chalet, a restaurant that formerly existed at 2201 Wilshire Boulevard. The restaurant's quaint interior had chairs with heart-shaped backs, a carved bear and a cuckoo clock, and must have reminded Mann of home. He recorded having eaten there fifty-six times in his diary, often with a 'good' or 'very good' appetite.

His regular lunch spot was the restaurant at the Fairmont Miramar Hotel, which exists to this day, as a luminous landscape of globe lighting and sinuous blue-velvet banquettes.

Mann's son Golo has commented that 'In a writer's house like my father's, the reality fluctuated, so to speak, and the artistic and the so-called real mixed in a strange way.' Yet still Mann was able to celebrate LA for its 'paradisiacal climate', according to Corngold. He once wrote, 'We do not lack good friends and good music, and if one did not constantly have the smell of the fire of world history in one's nostrils, and in one's ears the SOS call of the dying, life could be pleasant.'

Gabriel García Márquez

1927–2014

He spent his afternoons in cafés

Aureliano continued getting together in the afternoon with the four arguers, whose names were Álvaro, Germán, Alfonso and Gabriel, the first and last friends that he ever had in his life. For a man like him, holed up in written reality, those stormy sessions that began in the bookstore and ended at dawn in the brothels were a revelation.

– From *One Hundred Years of Solitude* by Gabriel García Márquez

During his later years, the Colombian writer and Nobel laureate Gabriel García Márquez became the most famous man in Latin America, best friend of the Cuban dictator Fidel Castro, and known to everyone by the one-word nickname 'Gabo'. But before his first novel, *One Hundred Years of Solitude*, catapulted him to international fame, he was just one of the pranksters associated with the bar La Cueva, part of a group of friends in the city of Barranquilla, Colombia, who got together every afternoon to drink and talk about everything under the sun: politics, the economy, sometimes even literature, depending on who you ask.

For García Márquez, spending time drinking and talking with his friends was a crucial part of his writing routine, which started at 5a.m. and ran until 2p.m. or so, when it became time to hang out in cafés. In Barranquilla, people met at the Mundo bookstore, the Japi bar and the now-legendary bar of La Cueva, which still exists as a restaurant to this day, but in the early 1950s, when García Márquez was living in Barranquilla, it was a grocery store with a dive bar attached. The book *Solitude & Company* by journalist Silvana Paternostro attempts to excavate the writer's life through oral history from those who knew him, including the friends from this era. La Cueva, one says, 'was like a house and there was like a little terrace. You went in and there was a bar, a folkloric bar, I mean with all kinds of hats, and then there were some armchairs and little tables.' It served beer, snacks and rum, and in addition to the writer and his circle, was patronized by the local crocodile-hunters. Another old friend recalls that 'we would order a bottle of white rum and a bottle of tamarind. A bottle of white rum and a bottle of tamarind cost 25 cents. And they added slices of lemon.'

Some of the friends from this era appear in *One Hundred Years of Solitude* as 'the four arguers', the friends of the book's hero Aureliano Buendía, and source of the famous quotation above. And though the author didn't have the 'a-ha' moment that allowed him to actually complete the novel until 1967, he was working endlessly on versions of the idea even in the early 1950s. Another old friend told Paternostro that 'Every day he'd write a new chapter and then he'd say to us: "Read this." Álvaro would say: "Don't fuck around, you have a lot of balls, this is shit!" I didn't read *One Hundred Years of Solitude* after it was published, but I read it two hundred thousand times because every day that madman would read the damn chapter he had written the night before.'

After the book's publication, everything changed. García Márquez won the Nobel Prize in Literature in 1982, and brought an entourage to Sweden the likes of which the awards ceremony had never seen: 150 people, including a troupe of *vallenatos* musicians, who played a kind of rustic folk music from the north of Colombia, which Bogota sophisticates considered tacky but the international audience loved. In Gabo's later years he dined on caviar and champagne, became friends with Castro – whom he once saw

LA
CUEVA

For García Márquez spending time drinking and talking with his friends was a crucial part of his writing routine.

sample eighteen different flavours of ice cream in one sitting – and even had dinner with Bill Clinton at the home of William Styron on Martha's Vineyard in August of 1994. (García Márquez wanted to discuss Cuba; Clinton wanted to discuss literature.) He treated friends to lunch and signed autographs in restaurants – once giving a young woman the money to run out and buy his latest book, a move of supreme confidence which assumed that of course his book would be in stock.

However, the man from the small town of Aracataca (fictionalized as Macondo in his work) stayed close to his roots in some ways. His legendary conversations with Castro – a later in life echo of the sessions with 'the four arguers' – were often homely discussions of things like the best way to prepare snapper, or why corn bread pairs so well with sour cream. Such details are reminiscent of his quotidian, mythic boyhood in Aracataca, where he lived with his grandparents in a house with an immense yard of fruit trees, including guava trees and a jackfruit tree inhabited by a sloth. The sloth would throw down the jackfruits and his grandmother would parboil them to eat. The town had no electricity, and at night people told stories by kerosene lamps and by candlelight. Later, García Márquez used the style of these stories in his fiction, and a legend was born.

Writers Who Didn't Eat Proper Meals

Bad dining habits and good writing go together like pen and ink

Philip Roth's autobiographical writer-hero Nathan Zuckerman observes early on in the Zuckerman series that the time and mental focus required to write well can be contrary to the life fully lived. Writers, Zuckerman thinks, need 'Purity. Serenity. Simplicity. Seclusion. All one's concentration and flamboyance and originality reserved for the grueling, exalted, transcendent calling.' Roth is making gentle fun of the typical writer's ego – but he's accurate about their habits. Many reserve all their energy for writing, and eat poorly as a result. Here are some of the worst.

Lewis Carroll: Crackers and Sherry
Lewis Carroll is on record as enjoying a full, hearty breakfast, and then skipping his midday meal in favour of 'a glass of wine and a biscuit' – probably sherry and a cracker in the modern parlance.

David Foster Wallace: Blondies
Wallace's addiction to caffeine and junk food was legendary, and he often lived on Pop Tarts and blondies, while keeping his refrigerator bare.

Marcel Proust: Two Croissants and Two *Cafés au Lait* a Day
Proust's housekeeper has written that the bed-confined writer survived on croissants and bowls of *café au lait* – in later years skipping the croissants entirely and just drinking the milky coffee.

Patricia Highsmith: Bacon, Eggs and a Stiff Drink
Like Proust, Highsmith also wrote in bed, but she started her day with a drink – perhaps gin, since gin martinis were her favourite – along with coffee and a doughnut. Otherwise she ate bacon and eggs for almost every meal.

William Somerset Maugham: Breakfast Three Times a Day
'To eat well in England, you should have breakfast three times a day,' the author and playwright is quoted as having said, presumably as a damning verdict on the English food of his era.

Edna St. Vincent Millay

1892–1950

A Maine-inspired menu

May 17, 1934
Ugin makes a beef bouillon & skims the fat off twice, then lets it come to a boil for just a few minutes. It is delicious, either served hot or in jelly. Then we make a salad with herbs in it, tarragon, & chives & sage, and a few leaves of spearmint.

– From *Rapture and Melancholy: The Diaries of Edna St. Vincent Millay*, edited by Daniel Mark Epstein

The poet Edna St. Vincent Millay had a haunted childhood, like something out of a fairy-tale. In 1904, her newly divorced mother Cora moved with her three daughters to salty, seaside Camden, Maine, on Penobscot Bay. Cora took the smallest house in the town's poorest neighbourhood, a dwelling down a flight of stairs on low ground, whose kitchen floor flooded and froze in the winter when the river was high. Yet the three Millay girls 'gleefully ice-skated across it', according to Millay biographer Nancy Milford. Cora left the sisters alone for long stretches while she worked, putting them in charge of the cooking, cleaning and going to the market, often on very little money. The sisters played games and sang songs – made up by Vincent, as she was called as a child – to make the work lighter, and presumably also to make their solitude less frightening.

The family stood out in town, with three young girls fending for themselves, but they weren't ashamed of it. Vincent made breakfast and drew up lists of chores and responsibilities ('Kathleen brings in wood for breakfast / Norma feeds Wuzzy / Vincent kills flies'). She was also expected to cook daily, bake several times weekly, and wash clothing for herself and her sisters. When staying on her Uncle Fred's farm, she was tasked with picking blueberries, and sometimes they all ate only blueberries and milk for dinner. Despite the family's difficult circumstances, Cora never hesitated to advocate for Vincent's genius with her teachers at school, and people in Camden remembered Millay as brilliant and sure of herself.

Her favourite foods, she wrote, were those of her Maine childhood: 'broiled or boiled Maine lobsters with melted fresh country butter, haddock chowder . . . and deep dish blueberry pie.'

Millay became famous at twenty years old for a poem she'd entered in a contest, 'Renascence', and later became a jazz-age bohemian feminist icon and winner of a Pulitzer Prize. Yet after a period of living in New York City and in Europe, she seemed to return to her roots. She married a motherly Dutchman named Eugen (Ugin) Jan Boissevain and bought Steepletop, a 635-acre blueberry farm near Austerlitz, New York, that must have been reminiscent of her uncle's. She lived there until her death in 1950, and the property is currently the site of the Millay Arts campus. As an adult Millay eschewed traditional female gender roles and hated chores, so Boissevain took care of the house. However, she liked to garden and grow vegetables, and the 2022 book *Rapture and Melancholy: The Diaries of Edna St. Vincent Millay* reveals an enviable lifestyle of fresh country foods, visits from friends and support from Boissevain. In April 1927, she wrote, 'Ugin brought up breakfast to Elinor & me in my bed & made a lovely fire in my fireplace.' And: 'Elinor, Gene & I drove down to Austerlitz in a snow-storm . . . went

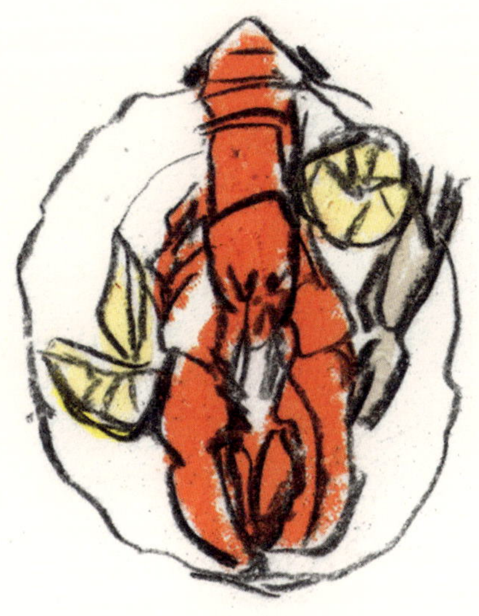

to Columbia Inn & drank muscatel & read mail.' A few days later, 'Had beautiful roast chicken ... but while we were talking with Max about the value, if any, of anthologies of verse, the onions burned on ... Opened one of the last jars of raspberries – incredibly fresh & delicious.' Her favourite foods, she wrote, were those of her Maine childhood: 'broiled or boiled Maine lobsters with melted fresh country butter, haddock chowder ... and deep dish blueberry pie'.

Millay had a complicated personal life (both she and Boissevain took other lovers), and she was plagued by health problems. The same series of diary entries from April of 1927 reports that once she 'Stayed in bed most all day, feeling mizzy', but then also got up in the afternoon to go to Albany with Ugin to take the guests to the train – in more blizzards. Upon return, the couple 'Opened one of the last jars of red strawberries – so good, so good!' Her capacity to appreciate the joys among her trials and sorrows served her well for all of her life.

Haruki Murakami

1949–present

Food as a link to reality

Nineteen-seventy-one was the Year of Spaghetti. In 1971, I cooked spaghetti to live, and lived to cook spaghetti. Steam rising from the pot was my pride and joy, tomato sauce bubbling up in the saucepan my one great hope in life.

– 'The Year of Spaghetti', published in *The New Yorker* in 2005

One of many online tributes to the food in Japanese author Haruki Murakami's novels, the Like Bears to Honey blog catalogues a list of all the meals across the three volumes of *1Q84*, finding twenty-six tantalizing scenes and quoting them in full, with humorous commentary about each. From the lavish (mussels, a three-onion salad and 'Bordeaux-braised Iwate veal stew') to the simple (tomato and wakame salad and a slice of toast), Murakami's descriptions of cuisine, sometimes Japanese but often not, have obsessed readers around the world, who wish to try the dishes for themselves. One fan has written a cookbook (Japanese-language only). One has written a food-focused guidebook to Murakami's Japan (Spanish-language only). And an art student at Cooper Union made an infographic showing the ingredients and techniques for the food in *1Q84*.

Part of the allure of these meals is how comforting they are. Murakami's focus on the seemingly banal but very specific details of a character's

Murakami's descriptions of cuisine, sometimes Japanese but often not, have made readers around the world obsessed and wishing to try the dishes for themselves.

day makes the reader feel like the character – and possibly life – is safe and familiar. One of the most iconic appearances of food in Murakami's work, in fact, is a food so familiar it's almost a joke: spaghetti. Yet as the story 'The Year of Spaghetti' develops, the spaghetti shimmers and changes on the page, becoming abundant and strange: 'Spaghetti alla parmigiana, spaghetti alla napoletana, Spaghetti al cartoccio, Spaghetti aglio e olio, Spaghetti alla carbonara, Spaghetti della pina,' the story intones, as the character cooks and cooks. The spaghetti begins to represent the character's inner life and emotional state, which is in turmoil no matter how plain he looks on the outside.

Another great Murakami food scene comes in the novel *The Wind-Up Bird Chronicle.* In it, the main character, Toru, goes through utterly ordinary elements of the daily grind, buying 'detergent, tissues, and toilet paper' before going home to lie on the sofa and read a book, followed by cooking dinner. Toru says: 'I would be stir frying thin slices of beef, onions, green peppers, and bean sprouts with a little salt, pepper, soy sauce, and a splash of beer – a recipe from my single days. The rice was done, the miso soup was warm, and the vegetables were all sliced and arranged in separate piles in a large dish, ready for the wok.' It's quotidian, but wonderful, because Murakami has a talent for making ordinary lives mysterious, strange and surreal. This is an author with whom you can spend 500 pages before the main character falls into a well and the plot wanders away, unexplained to the end. 'Murakami's descriptions of food do exactly what his novels do best – they take the mundane and make it somehow magical, take the real and warp it into a dream,' wrote Adrienne LaFrance in the pages of *The Atlantic* magazine. Sometimes the food details feel like 'the only thing anchoring the story to reality'.

The novel *Norwegian Wood* offers another possibility for the meaning of food in Murakami's work. The book's hero, also named Toru, is chronically depressed after a friend's suicide and the loss of a woman who seems like his soul-mate. His days are boring and meaningless, until he meets Midori, a young woman who cooks for him on their first date. Toru observes:

> I sipped my beer and focused on Midori as she went on cooking, her back to me. She worked with quick, nimble movements, handling no fewer than four cooking procedures at once. Over here she tested the taste of a boiled dish, and the next second she was at the cutting board, rat-tat-tatting, then she took something out of the refrigerator and piled it in a dish, and before I knew it she had washed a pot she was finished using. From the back, she looked like an Indian percussionist – ringing a bell, tapping a block, striking a water buffalo bone, each movement precise and economical, with perfect balance.

It's clear just from how Midori moves about the kitchen that she has the joy in life that Toru lacks. Murakami's plots tend towards darkness, confusion and mystery; his characters often find themselves wandering in surreal realities not quite fastened to daily life, yet he finds ways to ground the narrative in the simple and recognizable. Toru realizes that 'It's good when food tastes good, it's kind of like proof you're alive.'

Murakami's knack for describing food preparation possibly comes from experience. The writer's first career was as the owner of a jazz club. Shortly after college – in fact, a few credits short of graduation – he opened a small place near Tokyo's Sendagaya Station, and in the beginning was its sole employee. In his memoir, *What I Talk About When I Talk About Running*, published in English in 2008, he writes that he did everything: 'keeping accounts, checking inventory, scheduling my staff, standing behind the counter myself mixing up cocktails, and cooking . . .' In the early days of trying to be a novelist, he came home from work at the club and often sat up at his kitchen table writing until dawn.

Murakami says that he does not consider himself to be a likeable person. He says he is naturally solitary, and when he closed his bar to embark upon writing full time, he made the conscious choice not to interact with too many people, in order to have time for his work and to preserve his creative energies. For even more battery-recharging solitude, he likes long-distance running. In the period covered by the memoir, he was running six days a week for at least an hour, with a target of 156 miles per month.

It's an ascetic life, but it has its pleasures. Murakami reports that, like most of us, he has a tendency to gain weight when he's too sedentary. But, when living in Boston, he says he treats himself to Samuel Adams beer and Dunkin' Donuts, which he can do because he's running enough to keep his weight down. Mostly he's a healthy eater of clean, delicious-sounding food, a habit that formed naturally when he started running every day. 'I began to eat mostly vegetables, with fish as my main source of protein. I never liked meat much anyway, and this aversion became even more pronounced. I cut back on rice and alcohol and began using all natural ingredients. Sweets weren't a problem since I never much cared for them,' he writes. Hawaii, where he also lives part-time, is perfect for him because he 'can easily get lots of fresh fruits – mangoes, papayas, avocados – literally right across the street'.

When in Hawaii he likes to eat at the Hanalei Dolphin Restaurant, where he orders 'walu, a kind of white fish. They grill it for me over charcoal, and I eat it with soy sauce. The side dish is vegetable kebabs, plus a large salad.' The restaurant has been open since the early 1970s and is still in operation today, allowing fans who can make it to Hawaii to have a meal with Haruki Murakami, or at least in a place he has dined. Surreal.

The Six Greatest Dishes in Literature

Herman Melville's Clam Chowder
Work: *Moby-Dick*

See: entirety of the chapter 'Chowder'

Location served: The Try Pots Inn, Nantucket

Description: Ishmael and his friend Queequeg discover 'chowder for breakfast, and chowder for dinner, and chowder for supper' at the Try Pots Inn.

Quote: 'It was made of small juicy clams, scarcely bigger than hazel nuts, mixed with pounded ship biscuit, and salted pork cut up into little flakes, the whole enriched with butter, and plentifully seasoned with pepper and salt.'

Critical significance: *Moby-Dick* is considered to have homoerotic themes, and scholars have suggested that Ishmael and Queequeg were gay lovers. Their enjoyment of the bountiful chowder may represent the warmth and happiness of their relationship.

Verdict: 'Surpassingly excellent.'

Thomas Pynchon's Banana Breakfast
Work: *Gravity's Rainbow*

See: several pages early in the book, plus further allusions

Location served: Chelsea, London, during the Blitz

Description: Capt. Geoffrey 'Pirate' Prentice, a US Army captain stationed in London during the Second World War, makes a banana-themed breakfast for his messmates.

Quote: '. . . banana omelets, banana sandwiches, banana casseroles, mashed bananas molded in the shape of a British lion rampant, blended with eggs into batter for French toast, squeezed out a pastry nozzle across the quivering creamy reaches of a banana blancmange to spell out the words *C'est magnifique, mais ce n'est past la guerre* [...] tall cruets of pale banana syrup to pour oozing over banana waffles, a giant glazed crock where diced bananas have been fermenting since the summer with wild honey and muscat raisins, up out of which, this winter morning, one now dips foam mugs full of banana mead . . . banana croissants and banana kreplach, and banana oatmeal and banana jam and banana bread, and bananas flamed in ancient brandy Pirate brought back last year from a cellar in the Pyrenees also containing a clandestine radio transmitter . . .'

Critical significance: the banana, the penis and the rocket are symbolic of each other in *Gravity's Rainbow*, representing perhaps the powerful but absurd urge to make war.

Verdict: the soldiers 'dream drooling' of Pirate's breakfasts.

Haruki Murakami's Spaghetti

Work: 'The Year of Spaghetti', published in *The New Yorker*, 2005

See: about two pages; entirety of the story

Location served: a lonely man's apartment, possibly in Japan

Description: It's the year 1971 and a man makes a lot of spaghetti.

Quote: 'Fine particles of garlic, onion, and olive oil swirled in the air, forming a harmonious cloud that penetrated every corner of my tiny apartment, permeating the floor and the ceiling and the walls, my clothes, my books, my records, my tennis racquet, my bundles of old letters. It was a fragrance one might have smelled on ancient Roman aqueducts.'

Critical significance: Murakami is known for declining Japanese cultural markers in his fiction, shown here by the protagonist's fondness for spaghetti.

Verdict: 'Born in heat, the strands of spaghetti washed down the river of 1971 and vanished.'

Virginia Woolf's *Boeuf En Daube*

Work: *To the Lighthouse*

See: Chapters XVI and XVII

Location served: a beach house in the Isle of Skye, Inner Hebrides

Description: Mrs. Ramsay, a mother of eight mostly adult children, is hosting a summer gathering in the Hebrides, and serves *boeuf en daube* one evening for dinner, worrying that all the diners should be on time for the meal.

Quote: 'an exquisite scent of olives and oil and juice rose from the great brown dish'

Critical significance: in this semi-autobiographical work, Woolf was exploring the conflicting female roles of artist vs home-maker. The *boeuf en daube* is the kind of domestic triumph that Woolf's daughter-character eschews in favour of making art.

Verdict: 'It partook . . . of eternity . . . Of such moments, [Mrs. Ramsay] thought, the thing is made that endures.'

Giuseppi Tomasi di Lampedusa's *Timpano*

Work: *The Leopard*

See: a couple pages in the chapter 'Donnafugata'

Location served: Donnafugata, Sicily

Description: a *timpano* (or *timballo*) is a classic Italian showstopper dish of pasta baked in a large Dutch oven (*timbale*, in French), which has been lined with sheet pasta. Inverted and plated it resembles a drum. The aristocratic family portrayed in *The Leopard* serves it at a dinner.

Quote: 'The burnished gold of the crusts, the fragrance of sugar and cinnamon they exuded, were but preludes to the delights released from the interior when the knife broke the crust; first came a mist laden with aromas, then chicken livers, hard-boiled eggs, sliced ham, chicken, and truffles in masses of piping-hot, glistening macaroni, to which the meat juice gave an exquisite hue of suède.'

Critical significance: this lavish but traditional dish represents the hidebound decadence of the aristocracy.

Verdict: the *demi-glace* is too rich, but most of the diners find the *timpano* delicious.

Margaret Mitchell's Barbecue

Work: *Gone With the Wind*

See: the beginning of Chapter IV

Location served: Twelve Oaks Plantation, Georgia

Description: heroine Scarlett O'Hara, dressed in a low-cut 'afternoon dress' of green flowered muslin and showing 'two inches of green Morocco slippers', sits surrounded by *beaux* at the annual Twelve Oaks barbecue, not eating her plate of food because it would be improper for a young woman to show appetite, and longing for the only man who isn't paying her any attention: Ashley Wilkes.

Quote: 'The barbecue pits, which had been slowly burning since last night, would now be long troughs of rose-red embers, with the meats turning on the spits above them and the juices trickling down and hissing into the coals.'

Critical significance: critique of *Gone With the Wind* has long centred on Mitchell's stereotyped and racist portrayals of enslaved people and the barbecue scene is no exception. By positioning the barbecue, a traditional Black American practice, hidden far from the house, Mitchell displays the noxious attitudes towards race that were typical of her place and time.

Verdict: Scarlett doesn't take a bite.

FLOUR

Iris Murdoch

1919–99

Funny meals from cans

For lunch, I may say, I ate and greatly enjoyed the following: anchovy paste on hot buttered toast, then baked beans and kidney beans with chopped celery, tomatoes, lemon juice and olive oil. (Really good olive oil is essential, the kind with a taste, I have brought a supply from London.) Green peppers would have been a happy addition only the village shop (about two miles pleasant walk) could not provide them . . . Then bananas and cream with white sugar. (Bananas should be cut, never mashed, and the cream should be thin.) Then hard water-biscuits with New Zealand butter and Wensleydale cheese. Of course I never touch foreign cheeses. Our cheeses are the best in the world. With this feast I drank most of a bottle of Muscadet out of my modest 'cellar'. I ate and drank slowly as one should (cook fast, eat slowly) and without distractions such as (thank heavens) conversation or reading. Indeed eating is so pleasant one should even try to suppress thought.

– From *The Sea, The Sea* by Iris Murdoch

Charles Arrowby, the eccentric, unreliable narrator of Iris Murdoch's late masterpiece *The Sea, The Sea*, is known to all Murdoch fans for his peculiar meals, represented in the quotation above. Throughout the novel, Charles concocts strange-sounding repasts from cans and packets, and asserts preposterous rules, for example no meal should take more than four minutes to prepare, or that no one is allowed to mash their bananas. It's comedic, but also serves a literary purpose: Charles *claims* he has moved to the seashore to repent of a selfish and egotistical life – yet his gourmet blathering doesn't sound very repentant, and it is the first hint Murdoch gives the reader that he can't be trusted.

All the humour and whimsy of Charles's foodstuffs – though none of the dark side – came from Murdoch's life. Born in 1919 and educated at Somerville College, Oxford, Murdoch was a magnetic, mannish beauty who fell in love with both men and women, and who was often described as 'mysterious' by her various lovers. She and her husband, the literary critic John Bayley, had an unusual courtship, exchanging notes on drafts of each other's first novels over *vin rosé*, followed by an unusual open marriage that biographer Peter J. Conradi describes as 'legendarily happy'. Theirs was a union not of passion, but of playfulness and of the life of the mind.

These two otherworldly people bought a rambling, tumbledown country house in a small village outside Oxford, where they both taught. The house had no heat and leaked copiously, but Murdoch found it 'magical', Conradi says in *Iris: the Life of Iris Murdoch*, and loved to throw parties there. 'Iris and John were all the better hosts for seeming to be guests at their own parties,' Conradi wrote. The house was disastrously messy and the meals were questionable – John cooked, occasionally inedibly, or reheated food from the college dining hall. One evening, he served the critic A.N. Wilson a dish Wilson later described affectionately as 'tongue in green slime'. On another, Bayley talked up a 'surprise' dessert from Iris that turned out to be a packaged Mr Kipling cake (also reminiscent of an American Twinkie).

Conradi describes Bayley, who had an effervescent, easy charm, as Murdoch's 'child-wife'. Yet of the two, Bayley was the more practical. Murdoch's cooking and housekeeping were highly informal – friends of her youth recall her eating *their* food without really noticing; an anecdote from a student paints her munching on a cold baked potato while giving a lecture. Bayley ended up doing the housework and cooking, assembling picnic-like-dinners from cans in a fashion that Murdoch called 'Wind in the Willows'. He also stuffed his pockets with tidbits from the college dining hall to bring home to her. When the psychologist Anthony Storr asked Murdoch about Charles's weird food habits in *The Sea, The Sea*, she said, 'But this is what John and I eat *all the time*.'

The answer is a bit tongue in cheek, say Murdoch scholars Miles Leeson and Frances White, of the Iris Murdoch Research Centre at the University of Chichester in England. The couple went out to restaurants often, and 'certainly encountered better cuisine'. But both were resolutely casual in their dining habits. They liked to drink wine, but like Charles Arrowby, they refused to learn anything about it, and were famous for uncorking any bottle brought to their home – even those of great value – and pouring it on top of whatever plonk was already in their decanter. Arrowby made it a matter of principle: 'Why wantonly destroy one's palate for cheap wine?' he asks. 'One of the secrets of a happy life is continuous small treats, and if some of these can be inexpensive and quickly procured, so much the better.' Murdoch was one of the great philosopher-writers of the twentieth century, and these are words to live by.

'One of the secrets of a happy life is continuous small treats, and if some of these can be inexpensive and quickly procured, so much the better.'

LOL TA

Vladimir Nabokov

1899–1977

Beguiling with imagery

Lolita with her curved spine to Humburt, Humburt resting his head on his hand and burning with desire and dyspepsia . . . The latter necessitated a trip to the bathroom for a draft of water, which is the best medicine I know in my case, except perhaps milk with radishes, and when I reentered the strange pale-striped fastness where Lolita's old and new clothes reclined in various attitudes of enchantment on pieces of furniture that seemed vaguely afloat, my impossible daughter sat up and in clear tones demanded a drink too.

– From *Lolita* by Vladimir Nabokov

Vladimir Nabokov, author of one of literature's most notorious banned books, *Lolita,* was the eldest son of a wealthy and aristocratic Russian family displaced by the Revolution. In 1919, 'a flock of Nabokovs' – three families, as the writer explains in his autobiography *Speak, Memory* – fled from Russia to western Europe via the Crimea and Greece. They left behind a way of life that Nabokov was never to recapture, leaving the writer as a permanent exile with a schism in his heart between the culture of his birth and the places where he would eventually settle.

Nabokov wrote with nostalgia for this lost Russia, where one of his aristocratic mother's favourite pastimes while summering outside St Petersburg was 'the very Russian sport of *hodit po gribi* (looking for mushrooms)', which she'd collect in a basket 'stained blue on the inside by somebody's whortleberries'. She would sort, display and clean her collected treasures, and then direct them to be fried in butter and thickened with sour cream by her kitchen staff. Otherwise, the family's meals were planned by Nabokov's father, who would, '[w]ith a little sigh . . . open a kind of album laid by the butler on the dinner table after dessert and in his elegant, flowing hand write down the menu for the following day'.

What could ever measure up? In 1926, the newly married Nabokov wrote passionate love letters to his young wife Véra, destined to be his amanuensis and companion of his heart for more than fifty years until his death in 1977. As part of his commitment to tell her *everything* about his day, he noted the foods eaten at his German boarding house – which were a disappointment. The couple's collected letters were published in 2014 as *Letters to Véra*, translated and edited by Olga Voronina and Brian Boyd. Boyd told America's NPR that he thought these meals 'appealed very little' to the writer and that his descriptions of them 'quickly scrape the plate into the receptacle of the day's letter'. For example, on 3 June 1926 for lunch: 'They served me (in my room – as I asked) some broth with a rice-filled pastry, a lamb chop, and apple mousse.' And in the same letter, for dinner, in parentheses, '(fried eggs, fried potatoes with bits of meat, radishes, cheese, sausage)'. On 6 June 1926: 'For lunch they served broth with dumplings, meat roast with fresh asparagus, and coffee with cake.' On 11 June 1926: 'Lunch yesterday consisted of a veal chop and a banana in the company of cherries.' The writer bore this fare with a supreme indifference, because, as he also wrote to Véra on 24 January 1924, 'I am becoming more and more firmly convinced that *art is the only thing that matters* in life.'

Where food shone, for Nabokov, was in his art. The letters to Véra are full of lovely imagery, such as street lamps that burn with 'a warm and sweet lustre, like well-licked punch lollipops'. In *Lolita*, light is 'apple green' or his darling's lips are 'as red as a licked red candy'. When Humbert has a stolen orgasm with Lolita's legs on his lap, he says, '[t]he conjurer had poured milk, molasses, foaming champagne into a young lady's new white purse; an lo, the purse was intact' (i.e., she didn't know what had just happened). The ability to 'beguile with imagery . . . was a Nabokovian hallmark', Boyd told NPR.

In the scene quoted at the beginning of this chapter we see the deeper significance of food in *Lolita*. For Nabokov, an old-world European, the lure of Lolita is analogous to the lure of America: land of big cars, easy pleasures, gut-busting buffets and giant ice cream sundaes. But the pleasures are too much; the disordered indulgence makes you ill or mad. Thus, on the eve of Humbert's love's consummation, he has heartburn.

Véra was not a cook, and Nabokov never owned a house or made much of a home for himself. His final years, however, replicated life in his childhood mansion, when 'the kitchen and the servant's hall' were 'as far removed' from his mother's consciousness 'as if they were the corresponding quarters in a hotel', as he wrote in *Speak, Memory*. Famously, after the financial success of *Lolita*, Nabokov returned to Europe from America and took up residence on Lake Geneva – in the Montreux Palace Hotel, where he lived until his death, at home but never quite, as was his fate.

Pablo Neruda

1904–73

Food is poetry

Caldillo de Congrio (Conger Chowder)

Serves 4 as a main or 6 as a starter
• 3 garlic cloves • 3 tbsp olive oil • 1 small yellow onion, chopped • A handful of cherry tomatoes • ½ tsp ground cumin • 2 tbsp chopped fresh oregano • 875ml (30fl oz/3½ cups) fish stock (preferably homemade) • 120ml (4fl oz/½ cup) white wine • 8–10 small red new potatoes, skins left on and chopped in half • 450g (1lb) skinned conger eel medallions (or medallions of Chilean sea bass) • 225g (8oz/½lb) fresh prawns • 150g (5½oz/½ cup) shelled green peas • 1 egg yolk • 120ml (4fl oz/½ cup) double (heavy) cream • Salt and black pepper • Chopped fresh coriander (cilantro), to serve

First, make a garlic paste: in a mortar and pestle, pound the garlic together with the olive oil. Add the paste to a saucepan and sauté the paste with the onion and the cherry tomatoes. When the onion is soft and golden but not browned, add the cumin and oregano, and season with salt and pepper to taste.

Add the fish stock, white wine and the new potatoes and simmer until the potatoes are cooked through. Then add the conger eel or sea bass medallions and simmer until cooked, skimming the soup occasionally if need be. You can tell the eel is cooked when it begins to break down a little. At this point, break up the fish or eel with a fork, removing any bones. Add the prawns and green peas and simmer for a further 3 minutes, or until the peas are tender and the prawns are pink and cooked through. Turn off the heat.

In a separate bowl, whisk the egg yolk with the cream until combined, then add it to the soup and stir to combine. Top with chopped fresh cilantro, season to taste and serve.

– Adapted from 'Ode to Conger Chowder' by Pablo Neruda

Pablo Neruda might be literature's premiere writer of food poetry. The Chilean poet and politician, accepting the Nobel Prize in Literature in 1971, said that 'We [writers from the vast expanse of America] are called upon to fill with words the confines of a mute continent, and we become drunk with the task of telling and naming.' Neruda considered it his responsibility to 'tell about' and 'name' the riches of his continent and the things that mattered to ordinary people. As a politician, he was an idealistic representative of the people against the wealthy, the elite, the tyrants, and corruption and oppression in government. And as a poet he often sought to display the treasures of ordinary Chilean life. To this end he wrote an extraordinary series of tributes to natural or daily items such as bees, hummingbirds, lemons, tuna, artichokes, wine, oranges, seafood chowder, and even one to his socks.

'Ode to Tomatoes', originally published in his *Elemental Odes* volumes in 1954 and 1955, is exemplary of the genre. It starts with a vivid picture of city streets overflowing with tomatoes for sale in the bright summer sunshine. Using images of deceptive simplicity, and usually just one or two words per line, Neruda shows that the tomato is abundant and everywhere – 'its juice / runs / through the streets'. This common item also has powers we wouldn't quite expect. It 'invades' kitchens and 'takes its ease' on worktops and 'sheds / its own light'. Every Chilean kitchen can be host to its 'benign majesty' and 'living flesh'. The implication is that no matter how poor or humble a person is, they have easy access to the highest and most exalted forms of experience, such as the encounter with this 'star of earth / recurrent / and fertile / star'. A good tomato; a lemon; a glass of wine – Neruda urges readers to appreciate that life's most glorious things are often its most simple.

The poems are also filled with action and energy, bringing the Chilean people – and readers everywhere – into a living relationship with the ingredients. In 'Ode to Tomatoes', Neruda describes chopping up the tomato for a salad, and suggests it be seasoned with simplicity that needs

Neruda might be literature's premiere writer of food-poetry.

no adornment: just olive oil, pepper, salt and parsley. The 'Ode to Conger Chowder' mentioned above, gives such detailed instructions on how to prepare this regional dish that it has inspired a host of recipes on the internet. (The recipe, see page 145, is a combination of many of them. Unfortunately, the conger, a giant eel that can grow up to two metres in length, might be hard to track down.)

Neruda lived with the joy and urgency that he expressed in his poetry. He served his country as an ambassador, a representative of the Chilean Communist Party to the Chilean Senate, and in 1969, shortly before his death, as a presidential candidate. An Art of Poetry interview with *The Paris Review* just before he withdrew his candidacy in 1970 describes a 6,000-square-metre estate he purchased on the Isla Negra beachfront, forty kilometres south of Valparaiso, long before the area became popular. The estate was decorated with eccentric items from antique stores and junkyards, and Neruda entertained there frequently, mostly in a bar room styled to look like a ship's salon, 'with furniture bolted to the floor, and nautical maps and paintings'. He made the drinks himself. Meals at this estate in the summertime were served on a porch facing a garden that had an antique railroad carriage in it. The fare was typically Chilean – *The Paris Review* interview mentions 'fish with a delicate sauce of tomatoes and baby shrimp', *caldillo de congrio,* and meat pies. The wine served was always Chilean. One of the porcelain pitchers Neruda served it from was shaped like a bird and sang when the wine was poured. It could not have sung more sweetly though, than his 'Ode to Wine', which described the beverage as 'spiral-seashelled / and full of wonder, / amorous, / marine; / never has one goblet contained you, / one song, one man, / you are choral, gregarious, / at the least you must be shared …' The poem is a must for any wine-drinker, as Neruda's odes are for anyone who loves food.

Flannery O'Connor

1925–64

Writing was her 'filet mignon'

Peppermint Chiffon Pie

• ¾ cup evaporated milk • ¾ cup water • 3 eggs, separated • ⅛ teaspoon salt • whipped cream • 6 'Starlight Kisses' (peppermint candies made by Southern Home (or 1 oz. of any peppermint candies with corn syrup, sugar, and natural oil of peppermint) • 1 tablespoon plain gelatin • ¼ cup cold water • Keebler's Chocolate Ready Crust • chocolate syrup

Soak gelatin in cold water. Combine milk and water and scald in double boiler. Dissolve candy in warm, diluted milk. Beat egg yolks with ¼ cup sugar and add to scalded milk. Cook until mixture starts to coat spoon. Remove from heat and add gelatin. Set aside to cool. Beat egg whites until stiff but not dry while slowly adding ½ cup sugar. Carefully incorporate egg whites into the custard. Pour into chocolate shell and refrigerate. Spread whipped cream over top just before serving and dribble chocolate syrup over the cream.

– From documents kept at Andalusia Farm: home of Flannery O'Connor in Milledgeville, Georgia

Fried shrimp followed by peppermint chiffon pie was Flannery O'Connor's favourite lunch at the genteel Sanford House Tea Room in Milledgeville, Georgia, where O'Connor dined regularly with her mother throughout the 1950s. These were trying meals for O'Connor, a thin, awkward young woman who'd left Milledgeville in 1945 at age twenty for the Iowa Writers' Workshop. At Iowa, the devoutly Catholic young writer from the American South had impressed her professors and peers with fiction that programme director Paul Engle found 'imaginative, tough and alive', according to the biography *Flannery: A Life of Flannery O'Connor* by Brad Gooch. O'Connor quickly won the friendship of major figures of her day, such as the poets Robert Lowell and Elizabeth Hardwick, and found open doors to the Yaddo writers' retreat and the New York literary scene. However, a diagnosis of lupus in 1951 forced her home to Milledgeville, to live out the rest of her days in the loving but domineering clutches of her mother, Regina.

The Sanford House Tea Room 'wasn't her crew at all', biographer Gooch says. 'It was the ladies who lunch of Milledgeville.' During the meals, Regina was garrulous and O'Connor was silent, viewing it all with a satirist's eye. 'She was playacting as a member of this community whose pretension of decorum she saw through,' Gooch says. The experience was wonderful for her fiction, in which she often shows how characters' false propriety covers for evil and sin. But it was a frustrating life for a young woman.

O'Connor and her mother lived outside the town at Andalusia Farm, which was then a working farm and dairy that Regina ran with hard-nosed acumen and is now the Flannery O'Connor House Museum. When not dining out, O'Connor ate a 'curdled, dyspeptic plain kind of food', according to Gooch. In the mornings her mother would bring her a Thermos of coffee, then they'd go to morning Mass. After that, O'Connor would write for three hours – glorious time to herself that she 'ate up like filet mignon', as she wrote. Afternoons were for resting, correspondence and sitting on the porch. O'Connor and her mother rarely dined in the dining room, and her

O'Connor also particularly liked martinis and a 'Coca-Cola Black'—Coke mixed with black coffee.

letters refer to foods like cornflakes and canned sardines as ordinary fare. Regina's recipe for lemon chiffon pie, preserved in the Andalusia archives, has a hand-written note calling for more lemon juice to make it extra tart. O'Connor also particularly liked martinis and a 'Coca-Cola Black' – Coke mixed with black coffee.

Nonetheless, the American Southern tradition of fancy comfort food was a theme in O'Connor's life. When O'Connor was young, Regina hosted parties for her daughter's friends during Maurice Sendak radio broadcasts – a major event for the pre-television era – serving things like little sandwiches, pink cakes, home-made gingerbread, brownies and hot chocolate. And late in life, when O'Connor was in the hospital in Atlanta, Sanford House owner Mary Jo Thompson, a friend of Regina's, shipped O'Connor's favourite foods in to her. A note from May 1964 mentions a baked potato, shrimp salad, roast beef – and of course, the peppermint chiffon pie.

CHARCUTERIE SAINT-JACQUES

George Orwell

1903–50

The writer who washed dishes

Boiled Apple Dumpling

One of the best forms of suet pudding is the boiled apple dumpling. The core is removed from a large apple, the cavity is filled up with brown sugar, and the apple is covered all over with a thin layer of suet crust, tied tightly into a cloth, and boiled.

– From 'British Cookery' by George Orwell

While living in Paris in 1929, George Orwell discovered that on a tight budget of six francs a day, the only foods he could afford were bread and margarine or bread and wine, and even this simple diet was 'governed by lies'. Every day at mealtimes Orwell pretended to go out to a restaurant so his landlady and the people at his boarding house would not realize his destitution. Afterwards, he smuggled bread back to his room, bitterly wasting a franc a day on the more expensive rye loaves because they were round and easier to conceal in his pocket. In his hunger, he would look into shop windows, longing for the foods he saw there: whole dead pigs, baskets of hot loaves, great yellow blocks of butter, strings of sausages, mountains of potatoes, vast Gruyère cheeses.

The experience became the foundation for the introductory material in Orwell's great work on rough living, *Down and Out in Paris and London.* And food – and its availability to the working classes – remained of central concern to Orwell throughout his career. In a follow-up autobiographical work on his explorations of poverty and his turn towards socialism, *The Road to Wigan Pier*, Orwell wrote:

> A human being is primarily a bag for putting food into; the other functions and faculties may be more godlike, but in point of time they come afterwards. A man dies and is buried, and all his words and actions are forgotten, but the food he has eaten lives after him in the sound or rotten bones of his children. I think it could be plausibly argued that changes of diet are more important than changes of dynasty or even of religion . . . Yet it is curious how seldom the all-importance of food is recognized. You see statues everywhere to politicians, poets, bishops, but none to cooks or bacon-curers or market gardeners.

Orwell worked washing dishes in restaurant kitchens in Paris after his six-francs-a-day ran out, and *Down and Out in Paris and London* is, among other things, a monument to restaurant workers' lives. He also produced a monument to the middle- and working-class food of his era in the form of 'British Cookery', an essay on the dining habits of Britons, published in 1945 by the *Evening Standard.* Orwell condemned restaurant food: cheap restaurants were 'almost invariably bad' and expensive restaurants were 'almost invariably French or imitation French'. Instead he recommended the good British food served in private homes. The typical British breakfast, he said, was a three-course meal starting with porridge (coarse oatmeal 'sodden and boiled to a spongey mess' and best served with cream), followed by a meat or fish and then a toast course. Orwell's choice for a breakfast fish was the kipper, which is a herring 'split open and cured in wood smoke until it is a deep brown colour'. And the only acceptable toast-topping in his opinion was butter and orange marmalade.

The main meal of the day also followed a predictable pattern: meat, preferably roasted, a heavy pudding and a cheese. Orwell's enthusiasm for these good, plain foods shone through in his writing. The classic British 'joint' he describes as a large piece of meat such as a round of beef or leg of pork or mutton, roasted whole and surrounded by potatoes, which 'preserves a flavour and juiciness which meat roasted in smaller quantities never seems to attain'. He specifies doneness levels and slicing techniques and recommends sides such as Yorkshire pudding or a pudding made from suet (grated beef tallow) for the various cuts. And he had a special affection for potatoes cooked in particularly British ways, such as boiled in water 'containing a few leaves of mint' and served with butter poured over them.

In Orwell's novel *1984*, a bleak vision of a totalitarian future, the food is poor and even chocolate is rationed. The book's hero Winston works for the Ministry of Plenty, and when the ministry cuts the chocolate ration, it's his job to redact all documents relating to it. In real life, Orwell celebrated the good desserts found in middle- and working-class homes, claiming that 'puddings' are 'one of the greatest glories of British cookery'. He names three pudding classifications: suet puddings, pies and tarts, and milk puddings. Those made from suet crusts, he wrote, could be sweetened and boiled; or used as a casing for stewed fruits like apples or gooseberries; or covered with jam and rolled (a 'roly-poly pudding'); or merely eaten in slices with treacle poured over it. The recipe above is for his favourite, 'the boiled apple dumpling'.

SYLVIA PLATH
THE BELL JAR
SYLVIA PLATH
ARIEL SYLVIA PLATH

Sylvia Plath

1932–63

'How I love to cook . . .'

Rabbit à la Ted Hughes

Ted lit carbon fire, glowing to red coals in black oven . . . scraped carrots naked, cut onion, squashy tomato; cooked down strips of salt pork, floured pink tight rabbit flesh; seared rabbit to savory brown, chunked in big kettle; made rich dense gravy from drippings, adding flour, salt, boiling water, two packets of condensed soup - - - vegetable and beef and chicken, glass and a half of wine at Ted's insistence; added sauce to kettle with can of peas, onions, tomato & carrots. Boiled and bubbled . . .

– From *The Unabridged Journals of Sylvia Plath*, edited by Karen V. Kukil

Inside Sylvia Plath's journals from July of 1957, she made notes on ideas for possible stories she might write, including one called 'The Day of the Twenty-Four Cakes' about a woman who is at the end of her rope with her husband and children, and is wavering between running away and committing suicide. Instead, the woman will be 'stayed by need to create an order' and will 'slowly, methodically' begin to bake cakes, one for every hour in the day. The idea made its way into the visually stunning 2003 movie *Sylvia*, presented as a real biographical event. It wasn't, but it might well have been. Plath loved to cook in the same way she loved to write, as a celebration of the world, and as a personal artistic accomplishment. And at the same time, sometimes she worked too hard.

The tension between feeling overwhelmed versus believing that daily domestic work, like cooking, saved her was a major theme in the life of a writer and poet who struggled with depression and committed suicide in 1963 at only thirty years old. 'The abstract kills, the concrete saves . . . How dusting, washing daily dishes, talking to people . . . helps,' she wrote in January 1959. Often, she was able to celebrate the joys of cooking – she read Irma S. Rombauer's 1931 classic *The Joy of Cooking* 'like a rare novel', referred to it as 'my blessed Rombauer', and exclaimed 'How I love to cook' in one journal entry while lauding its recipes. And her frequent diary notations on food give a sense of her sensual and often joyous life with husband Ted Hughes. On honeymoon in Spain in 1956, she wrote about a birthday lunch of 'tuna and beans in cream sauce', eaten with a 'new green honeydew melon'. She describes the melon flesh poetically as 'sweet the way sunlight would taste, coming through the clear glassy green bulk of waves'. Plath also frequently notes the couple's breakfasts: coffee con leche for her, brandy-milk for Ted, eaten with 'bananas and sugar' (22 July); or, later, raisin bread and hot tea 'with the crisp fruity toast, sogged in butter' (15 June 1959). On the other hand, she saw a conflict between her domestic life and her writing work. Also on honeymoon, she wrote: 'I am getting worried about becoming too happily stodgily practical; Instead of studying Locke, for instance, or writing . . . I go make an apple pie . . . Whoa, I said to myself. You will escape into domesticity & stifle yourself by falling headfirst into a bowl of cookie batter.'

Plath biographer Linda Wagner-Martin writes of 'the strain to be excellent at everything she did' that afflicted Plath, and about her 'almost obsessive need to live the perfect life, love the perfect man, create the perfect household, as a means of proving that she was a success in all the areas women were supposed to excel in'. Plath enjoyed boasting about her cooking, writing at one point that she made a 'damn good' lemon meringue pie, and discussing her tricks for doing so without refrigeration (cooling the crust and the custard on a cold bathroom window-sill). And the precision and deliciousness of her meal descriptions in her diaries are an inspiration. On 31 May 1959, she had: 'A supper, light and delectable, of ham, succulent with fat and cloves and crust, asparagus, and a thread-thin noodle cooked in chicken broth and browned with cheese and bread crumbs. Vanilla ice cream, fresh strawberries and finger-size jelly rolls for dessert.' On 26 March 1956: 'juicy tomato salad & celeri, sardines & a fine pear cold as honey for dessert'. The reader can feel her enjoyment when she writes about 'hungrily putting the last minutes of cooking onto breaded veal in cream, green parsley rice and rather soggy yellow squash'.

However, in that same entry she mentions that she is 'very weary'. Hughes and Plath bought a dream home in a village in Devon in 1961, an ancient ten-room house with a wine cellar, a small attic and a cobblestone courtyard out front that adjoined a churchyard and a cemetery. The house had a 'wilderness' of a back yard with seventy apple and cherry trees and blackberry and raspberry bushes. It sounds idyllic, but by this point Plath had a first baby and a recent miscarriage and was feeling the strain of motherhood while also trying to work on her own writing. She also had a tempestuous relationship with Hughes, whom she found out later was unfaithful to her. On an annotated calendar in 1962, with one child under two to care for and a new baby, Plath kept desperate lists of the things she accomplished or wanted to accomplish. 'The lists mushroomed,' Wagner writes, 'items from a week before or a day before appearing repeatedly.' The calendar reveals that in a single week, she made spaghetti, lemon pie, banana bread, stew, rhubarb and cupcakes.

Plath loved to cook in the same way she loved to write, as a celebration of the world, and as a personal artistic accomplishment.

Like the character in 'The Day of the Twenty-Four Cakes', Plath may have been trying to save herself with ambitious feats of cooking, but she wasn't successful. She knew that she needed to 'get rid of the accusing, never-satisfied gods who surround me like a crown of thorns', as she wrote in a diary entry, but she still thought that work and more work would help. A late diary entry reads: 'Very depressed today. Unable to write a thing. Menacing gods. I feel outcast on a cold star, unable to feel anything but an awful helpless numbness. I look down into the warm, earthy world. Into a nest of lovers' beds, baby cribs, meal tables, all the solid commerce of life in this earth, and feel apart, enclosed in a wall of glass.' The metaphor echoes her most famous one, of depression as a glass bell jar that descends upon the sufferer and cuts her off from the world. The woman who wrote so well of both life and despair – who wanted babies, and made pies and refrigerator cheesecakes, and wanted to 'come into the right, rich full-fruited world of middle age' – was not able to escape her demons. However, her posthumous success and enduring legacy testify to how her story continues to resonate with women. She was not alone.

The Best Writing Snacks According to Six Writers

Agatha Christie
A cup of cream

Stephen King
A slice of cheesecake

F. Scott Fitzgerald
Tinned meat and apples

Michael Creighton
Ham and cheese sandwich and a Coke

Victor Hugo
Coffee and two raw eggs

Oscar Wilde
Champagne

Barbara Pym

1913–80

A culinary historian's dream

Toad-in-the-Hole

• 110g (⅔ cup) flour • 2 eggs • 300ml (1 cup) milk • ½ teaspoon salt • Butter for the baking dish • 225g (½ pound) sausages

In a large mixing bowl, whisk together the eggs, milk and salt. Add flour and whisk until incorporated. Set aside. Preheat oven to 220°C (425°F), butter a medium glass baking dish, add the sausages, and allow them to brown lightly in the oven, 5–7 minutes. Flip the sausages, pour the batter over them, return to oven, and continue cooking for about 40 minutes, until batter has risen and set and the sausages are well-browned.

– Valerie Stivers

For her first evening meal in the WRNS (Women's Royal Naval Service) on 7 July 1943, as reported in her autobiography *A Very Private Eye*, English domestic-comedy writer Barbara Pym ate Toad-in-the-Hole, a humble, homey dish of sausages cooked in Yorkshire pudding batter, served with a side of 'bread and jam'. The Pym of the era was a tall, attractive girl, unhappy in love and unhappily thwarted in her attempts to get a first novel published. She'd joined the WRNS not from patriotic fervour but as an attempt to change the scenery and forget a broken heart, one of many in her lifetime. (Diary snippet: 'I still love him as much as ever, and nothing will alter that except meeting somebody else.') But she was often homesick, and her diary reveals her longingly counting the days until furloughs and weeping during reunions with family and friends. This recipe, which she and her sister often made for dinner, was a taste of home.

Pym liked to cook and eat, and she always had a sense of humour about food – in one letter written from the WRNS she noted that while they had plenty of it, they sometimes had a long wait for their cutlery. And when she did achieve literary success in 1950, foods from simple Toad-in-the-Hole to sophisticated sole Nantua made appearances in her novels. Specifics about meals were such a frequent feature in her books that her sister Hilary Pym and her close friend, cookbook author Honor Wyatt, compiled *The Barbara Pym Cookbook* after Pym's death. 'This book may not come as a surprise to readers of my sister's novels,' Hilary wrote, since the novels contain many references to 'carefully prepared meals (successful or unsuccessful), restaurant lunches, gourmet dishes, solitary suppers (actual or in prospect), Sunday family dinners, packed lunches and party food, teas of all kinds, breakfasts large and small . . .'

More than just enjoying her food, Pym found in it the inspiration to write.

The foods that Pym ate, as represented in the cookbook and her voluminous journals, are wide-ranging and demonstrate a tension found in her life between cosy domesticity and foreign glamour (the latter usually referenced tongue-in-cheek). Recipes in the cookbook for dishes like asparagus mousse, potted ham, kipper pâté and boiled chicken (a traditional meal to serve to a new curate, she notes) represent her cultural grounding in notoriously plain English fare. But she also tried foreign foods; she was known to hand-make ravioli, and used grape leaves growing on the house she shared with her sister at Brooksville Avenue, London NW6, to make dolma. In 1966, when a coach service started up between London and Athens (four nights on the road), Pym and Hilary were 'among the first' to sign up. Hilary includes a recipe for a Greek egg-and-lemon soup in the cookbook to commemorate their trip.

Pym did not just enjoy her food and dining, it also served her the inspiration to write. She kept abundant diaries and often sat in public, especially in restaurants, taking notes on the people she saw, including their looks, dress and what they were eating, according to food historian Laura Shapiro in an essay on The Barbara Pym Society website. The restaurant Lyons Corner House in London was her favourite place to sit and observe, Shapiro says, and when Pym looked at a pair of shoes or a piece of cake, she saw indications of someone's personality, social class and emotional state. After a spell of popularity in the 1950s, Pym was dropped by her publisher in 1963 and spent many years in obscurity before being rediscovered in 1977. During that period, Shapiro writes, Pym still 'couldn't stop' jotting down observations, despite no longer being able to use them for published works. In one diary entry, she notes: 'Mr. C in the Library . . . He is having his lunch, eating a sandwich with a knife and fork, a glass of milk near at hand,' and then adds, 'Oh why can't I write about things like that any more . . . ?'

Pym's diaries were full of close observations of this nature, making her 'a culinary historian's dream', as a BookPage review of Shapiro's book, *What She Ate: Six Remarkable Women and the Food That Tells Their Stories*, says. And when her interest in the true-to-life detail found its way into her books, she knew she'd found her metier. While revising *Some Tame Gazelle*, her first novel to be published, she wrote in her diaries: 'More household detail . . . Knitting patterns . . . doing the alter flowers . . . Jam . . . ' After the word 'Jam' she penned in: 'Victoria plum 1907 with mould on top'. And thus a genius of domestic comedy was born.

George Sand
1804–76

A little fish, a chicken wing, ice cream and coffee

Chicken À La Jeune Fille

Fill a chicken with very fresh oysters, put in a hermetically sealed earthenware or iron vessel, boil until cooked in a bain-marie, add to the juice two ounces of butter, half a cup of milk, three hard boiled eggs chopped with parsley and a little starch, and cook, then with this mixture cover the chicken.

– From *À la Table de George Sand* by Christiane Sand

'There is not a more tranquil or a happier individual in his domestic life than this old troubadour retired from business,' George Sand, taking the masculine pronoun, wrote to her affectionate correspondent Gustave Flaubert in January of 1869. Sand, the pen-name for Amantine Lucile Aurore Dupin de Francueil, Baroness Dudevant, had earned her retirement. She'd published seventy novels in her lifetime and at one time was the most popular writer in all of Europe. She'd also survived a precarious early life and a tempestuous youth to become the happily settled grande dame of her family estate of Nohant, south of Paris. At Nohant, Sand lived with her children and grandchildren, and occupied herself with babysitting her little granddaughters, sewing their costumes for various theatricals, and attending to her correspondence. She seemed happy. In another letter to Flaubert from the same period, she writes, 'Played charades, had supper, and frolicked till daylight.' Later, 'I dine on a little fish, a chicken wing, an ice and a cup of coffee, never anything else, by which means my stomach keeps well.'

Sand may have been an abstemious diner but she ran all aspects of the estate at Nohant, and her devoted granddaughter, Aurore Lauth-Sand, saved an archive of 858 recipes that were in use during Sand's tenure overseeing the estate. A French-language book, published in 1987, *À la Table de George Sand,* offers an edited and streamlined collection of 245 of these recipes along with notations about which family member was their source. Many come from Sand's daughter-in-law; some come from illustrious guests such as Alexandre Dumas fils, son of the writer of *The Three Musketeers.* The recipes are arranged in traditional categories, such as sauces, soups, mains, eggs and so on, and betray many Continental influences, with Greek-style rice, *Charlotte Russe*, and a recipe for Italian gnocchi, which is the only one written in Sand's own hand. Originals of the recipes are written on all kinds of 'loose leaves, bundles, or on small notebooks deprived of their cover', the book reports, and the oldest are from Sand's grandmother, Marie-Aurore de Saxe, the first of the family to take ownership of Nohant.

The book also describes the estate's dining room: grey-painted woodwork, a white and grey tiled floor, colourful wall hangings, Louis XIV sideboards, presumably the setting for regular celebratory meals with Sand's many literary and artistic guests. The table setting included sumptuous white linens embroidered with the crest of the Marechal de Saxe, Sand's grandmother. Nearby, the huge kitchen had an open fire with a spit in front for roasting meat, along with a bread oven that turned out fresh bread daily and baked tarts made with fruit from the estate's orchards. The kitchen ceiling was reinforced with weathered beams and hung with pots, cauldrons, copper jam basins, and frying pans and saucepans arranged in order of size. Sand seems unlikely to have cooked anything herself in this wonderful milieu, but she loved making jam, and once joked that it was as important as writing novels.

Biographer Curtis Cate has said that Sand may well have been 'the most meticulously documented woman in 19th Century France'. Sand's many

letters, collected in a twenty-six-volume edition edited by Georges Lubin, portray a woman of strong passions and strong sorrows. In her youth, she was a rebel and socialist who wore trousers, smoked in the street, and demanded the bohemian freedom for a woman to follow her heart in matters of love. She entertained at Nohant from the beginning, even during her unhappy marriage, writing in 1827 about a party for over 100 people, where 'I gave superb feed to the whole commune, and we danced the bourée until two o'clock in the morning'. In her middle years she spent more and more time at Nohant and less in Paris, and provided hospitality and refuge for her many illustrious friends and lovers. Frédéric Chopin, one of the most famous of her lovers, stayed and worked there in the summers from 1839–45; the padded doors that Sand had installed on the room where Chopin composed are still on view at the estate, which is open to the public via guided tours in French.

The huge kitchen had an open fire with a spit in front for roasting meat, along with a bread oven that turned out fresh bread daily and baked tarts made from fruit from the estate's orchards.

Unfortunately, no notations survive of particular dishes served and to whom from Sand's many house parties. But we do learn about Flaubert's reciprocal trick for combatting an upset stomach in the collected letters he wrote, 'For my part, when I am not hungry, the only thing I can eat is dry bread. And the most indigestible food, such as apples in sour cider, and bacon, are what cure me of the stomach-ache.'

The 'Donkey Skin' Cake

Cake d'Amour
Preheat your wood-burning oven and butter a shallow dish. Put four large handfuls of flour in a bowl and make a well in the centre. Add four eggs, whisk to combine, then pour in a bowl of cream-topped milk. Sprinkle with sugar and mix to combine. Add a handful of butter, a pinch of baking powder, a drop of honey and a dash of salt. Knead, slipping in a ring to give your beloved while you do so. Bake for 1 hour.

– Adapted from *Peau d'Âne*

Frenchman Charles Perrault (1628–1703) was an early writer of fairy-tales, called *conte de fées*. The designation 'fairy' for popular folk-tales was coined in the Paris of his time by salon-denizen and writer Marie-Catherine Le Jumel de Barneville, Baroness d'Aulnoy. Perrault's versions of *Cinderella* and *Sleeping Beauty* are still popular, and his tale *Peau d'Âne* (Donkey Skin) is the inspiration for a cult classic 1970 French musical/fantasy movie directed by Jacques Demy.

In the movie, a princess disguised in a magic donkey skin flees an amorous father who wants to marry her – and of course she encounters her own Prince Charming along the way. The father is played by Jean Marais and the princess by a very young Catherine Deneuve. The trippy, singsong score was written by Michel Legrand. In a crucial scene near the end of the movie, Deneuve, singing, makes her beloved a '*cake d'amour*' after first flipping through her recipe book and deciding against other desserts, like apple savarin, rum pastry, walnut delight and royal cream puffs. Her method, translated above, seems more likely to produce a travesty, but needless to say the cake works, and she gets her fairy-tale ending.

Gertrude Stein

1874–1946

& Alice B. Toklas

1877–1967

Cubist cooking

Haschich Fudge

(*which anyone would whip up on a rainy day*)

Take 1 teaspoon black peppercorns, 1 whole nutmeg, 4 average sticks of cinnamon, 1 teaspoon coriander. These should all be pulverized in a mortar. About a handful each of stoned dates, dried figs, shelled almonds and peanuts: chop these and mix them together. A bunch of *cannabis sativa* can be pulverized. This along with the spices should be dusted over the mixed fruit and nuts, kneaded together. About a cup of sugar dissolved in a big pat of butter. Rolled into a cake or cut into pieces or made into balls about the size of a walnut. It should be eaten with care. Two pieces are quite sufficient.

– From *The Alice B. Toklas Cook Book* by Alice B. Toklas

'I do inevitably take my comparisons from the kitchen because I like food and cooking and I know something about it,' says Alice B. Toklas in *The Autobiography of Alice B. Toklas* by Gertrude Stein. Toklas was Stein's 'secretary-companion' (read: lifelong romantic partner), and the lovely conceit of the *Autobiography* is that by writing as Toklas, Stein reveals herself, her partner and their historically significant shared life.

Stein isn't read as much as she should be today, but she considered herself to be the foremost literary talent of her time – a claim with some grounds in reality. In *Stranger Than Fiction: Lives of the Twentieth-Century Novel*, the *New York Review of Books*' Classics editor Edwin Frank writes that she '[freed] American literature to be itself'. What's indubitable is that in Paris at the turn of the last century, she was in on the ground floor of the modern art movement, a collector and friend of Matisse and Picasso before they were famous, and a hostess of a great salon where all the talents of the day met and mingled. Between the wars, she mentored writers like F. Scott Fitzgerald and Ernest Hemingway.

The Autobiography of Alice B. Toklas, published in 1933, tells the story in Stein's métier of words. *The Alice B. Toklas Cook Book*, published in 1954, does it through Toklas's speciality: food. Toklas arrived in Paris in 1907, when Stein was living at 27 rue de Fleurus, in a small, two-storey home with an adjoining atelier hung with Stein's prescient and shocking collection of modern art. At that time, Stein's cook Hélène made dinner for the weekly Sunday night parties. The *Autobiography* is full of wonderful food details, such as one explaining that the quintessentially French Hélène disliked Matisse. She thought he had poor manners, so naturally she retaliated. 'Monsieur Matisse is staying for dinner this evening, she would say, in that case I will not make an omelette but fry the eggs. It takes the same number of eggs and the same amount of butter but it shows less respect and he will understand.'

Stein and Toklas are discreet. We don't learn when the latter takes over the kitchen at 27 rue de Fleurus (usually supervising a cook, of course), but the *Alice B. Toklas Cook Book* is a treasure trove of unusual recipes and well-researched techniques compiled by a woman who clearly spent a lifetime concerning herself with food. Toklas shows mastery of classic French items like *quenelles*, and has a sharp eye for an unusual recipe: a 'lemon salad' and 'Chinese eggs' from Sir Francis Rose, 4th Baronet of the Montreal Roses, for example. (The abbreviation 'Bart' is short for 'Baronet'.) For the former, you boil the lemons in brine then chop them up whole and serve with artichokes and salted almonds. For the latter, the eggs are boiled, then boiled in sherry, then baked with butter and soy.

Toklas's cookbook became an icon of the 1960s counterculture for its recipe for 'Haschich Fudge', see above. It was also the inspiration for the 1968 movie starring Peter Sellers, *I Love You, Alice B. Toklas*. The recipe caused controversy on the book's initial publication and was not included in the original American edition. Toklas claimed innocence, though one suspects falsely, since she writes that the fudge would be 'an entertaining refreshment for a Ladies' Bridge Club or meeting of the DAR' (Daughters of the American Revolution) and admits that 'euphoria and brilliant storms of laughter; ecstatic reveries and extensions of one's personality on several simultaneous planes are to complacently be expected'.

The *Alice B. Toklas Cook Book* is a treasure-trove of unusual recipes and well-researched techniques compiled by a woman who clearly spent a lifetime concerning herself with food.

One of Toklas's greatest observations, however, comes not in her cookbook, but in the *Autobiography*, where she claims that Matisse 'used his distorted drawings as a dissonance is used in music or as vinegar or lemons are used in cooking or egg shells in coffee to clarify'. Comparisons from the kitchen, it turns out, can have quite a bit to say about modern art.

Leo Tolstoy

1828–1910

He founded soup kitchens

Sour Schi from Fresh Cabbage

Boil a white bouillon with scraps of root and a handful of greens, a bay leaf, and a dozen peppercorns; and strain. Pour water over 10 sour small wild apples and cook separately until they are soft. Peel a small head of cabbage, chop finely, salt, squeeze out the liquid with your fists, add the cabbage to the strained bouillon and boil well. Then, pour in the liquid from the boiled apples to taste. Shortly before dinner, take 1 tablespoon butter, melt in a saucepan, add 1 finely chopped onion and gently fry, then pour in two tablespoons of flour and stir. Add this mixture to the cabbage soup, along with ½ to 1 cup of sour cream.

– Adapted from *A Gift to Young Housewives* by Elena Molokhovets

Early in the novel *Anna Karenina*, the character Levin, a salt-of-the-earth Russian landowner who has a passion for farming and for the welfare of his peasant workers, dines in a fashionable restaurant with the decadent Prince Stepan Arkadyevich Oblonsky. The prince orders three dozen oysters and a succession of dishes off the restaurant's French menu. Levin says he'll eat whatever but he prefers simple Russian dishes: *kasha* (a porridge made from buckwheat groats) and *schi* (a cabbage soup). The waiter absurdly butts in offering *Buckwheat à la Russe* (i.e. *kasha*, but in French). Tolstoy's intention is to satirize decadent and European trends in Russian society – his heart is with Levin.

Tolstoy was a Russian aristocrat, but after a brief period of extravagance in his youth he began to develop radical social theories that would evolve throughout his lifetime, which included a reverence for farming, militant vegetarianism and an anarchist opposition to the State. In the foreword to an 1892 Russian translation of an influential Victorian-era work on vegetarianism, *The Ethics of Diet*, he wrote that 'fasting is an indispensable condition of a good life' and laid out his belief that self-control in terms of the passions and appetites is the foundation of morality. Eating animals in particular was abhorrent, he believed, because we override our natural human identification with other living creatures, and our natural 'fear' of killing, for reasons of greed. Tolstoy was an early proponent of vegetarianism, his correspondence with a young Mahatma Gandhi may have helped shape the latter's thoughts. He wrote in the same work that 'a man who eats too much cannot strive against laziness, while a gluttonous and idle man will never be able to contend with sexual lust'.

Tolstoy also embraced a traditional Russian health cure involving *koumiss*, or fermented mare's milk. One summer he transported his entire huge family to land he owned outside of Samara in west-central Russia, where a Bashkir herdsman and his many veiled wives were summoned to live nearby and to make the *koumiss*, served daily in cups of Karelian Birch. However, he didn't always follow his own dour advice. A 2016 cookbook called *Leo Tolstoy: A Vegetarian's Tale* by S. Pavlenko, which draws on recipes and notes from the diaries of Tolstoy's wife, Sophia, quotes her worrying about the huge quantities of food her husband consumes, and declares that some of the egg dishes served at their estate of Yasnaya Polyana were 'quite extravagant': Sophie Tolstaya's 'scrambled eggs' called for eight eggs, 600 grams of sour cream, and two tablespoons of flour, for example.

Posterity is replete with contradictory material on Tolstoy's behaviour, which has long undermined his moral authority, though sometimes unfairly – knowing what is right and doing it are two different things. Fortunately, he recognized a great evil in November 1891, when a famine broke out in

Tolstoy was an early proponent of vegetarianism, and his correspondence with a young Mahatma Gandhi may have helped shape the latter's thoughts.

south-western Russia. Despite his radical principles, Tolstoy used his fame and Sophia's connections to raise money. With some of his children he travelled to the region, bought firewood and organized the baking of brown bread. Within a month he had opened thirty kitchens supplying free food to 1,500 people and he continued to expand his operations for the two years of the famine's duration. Sophia's diary, quoted in Henri Troyat's authoritative *Tolstoy* biography, describes the scene: 'The woman in charge offers each in turn a tray full of rye bread cut in pieces, then sets a big soup tureen full of cabbage soup on the table. There is no meat in it, and it has a mild taste of hemp oil . . . After the soup there is potato mash or peas, kasha, beet greens or barley porridge. Two dishes at noon, two at night.' Tolstoy was persecuted by the Russian government for calling attention to the famine, though ultimately not punished because of his fame and connections.

The cabbage soup above is from a legendary 1861 Russian cookbook and has been adapted to be vegetarian. The book's original instructions suggest serving soups of this nature with 'hard boiled or stuffed eggs, buckwheat *kasha*, *vatrushki* with *tvorg*, and *blini* layered with beef and brains'. Tolstoy wouldn't approve, but sometimes he *was* wrong.

Laura Ingalls Wilder

1867–1957

She ran a B&B serving good country food

Vinegar Pie with Sugared Cranberries

Serves 10

For the sugared cranberries:

• 225g (1 cup) sugar • 240ml (1 cup) water • 300g (2 cups) fresh cranberries • 50g (¼ cup) large-grain sugar, for rolling • 50g (¼ cup) small-grain sugar, for rolling

Combine the water and sugar in a small saucepan, and bring to a boil. Once it has boiled, remove from the heat, and let cool. Pour the liquid over the cranberries, and refrigerate overnight. Drain the cranberries. Working quickly so cranberries don't dry out, roll them first in large-grain sugar and then in small-grain sugar. Spread out on a plate to dry.

For the pie:

• 1 pre-baked pie crust of your choice • 2 eggs, beaten • 110g (½ cup) white sugar • 110g (½ cup) packed brown sugar • 50g (¼ cup) flour • A pinch of nutmeg • 3 tbsp raw unfiltered apple cider vinegar • 600ml (2½ cups) homemade whipped cream

In a large bowl, blend flour, nutmeg, and both sugars with your fingers until no lumps remain. Add vinegar, eggs, and the water, and stir until well mixed. Pour the filling into the prepared pie shell, and bake for 30–40 minutes, until set. Remove and chill. Top the chilled pie with a liberal layer of whipped cream and a pretty mound of sugared cranberries.

– Adapted from a recipe by Valerie Stivers for *The Paris Review*

Everyone who grew up on Laura Ingalls Wilder's classic novels of the American pioneer era, the Little House on the Prairie books, has their own particular treasured food memory from them. How Pa butchered the pig, smoked the meat, and used every bit of it, down to inflating the empty bladder for the girls to play with as a balloon. Or when the Ingalls family ran out of food at Plum Creek and ate only fried fish and 'crisp, juicy' turnips. Or Ma frying 'vanity cake' doughnuts, so-named because they're 'all puffed up, like vanity, with nothing solid inside'. Or Almanzo stuffing himself from the following spread at the county fair: pumpkin pie, custard pie, vinegar pie, mince pie, berry pie, cream pie, raisin pie . . .

So it's a hearty surprise to learn just how different Wilder's life was from the romanticized homesteader tales portrayed in the series. Writer Caroline Fraser's biography of Wilder, *Prairie Fires: The American Dreams of Laura Ingalls Wilder*, won a Pulitzer Prize for Biography in 2018, and offers revelatory context. What seemed like fun adventures to child readers were actually a desperate struggle for survival. Homesteaders like Pa, Fraser writes, 'could not succeed, no matter how hard they worked'. In the late 1800s, when the books are set, the American landscape was already suffering the beginnings of the environmental collapse that eventually created the droughts and dust storms of the 1930s. 'Virtually all the land best-suited to small-scale agriculture in the United States had been taken, and what was left was marginal,' Fraser wrote. 'Wilder never came to terms with what FDR saw and explained so clearly: the land had limits, and no solitary, undercapitalized farmer could ever hope to overcome them.'

Bowing to reality, in 1894 Laura Ingalls Wilder and husband Almanzo (Manly) moved from De Smet, South Dakota, to the more fertile Missouri Ozarks. There, Wilder raised chickens, drove a Model T Ford, and took many jobs to supplement the couple's income from farming. For a time she hosted summer boarders and did all the cooking herself, shunning fancy meats or canned goods, and supplying 'homemade country fare', her

For a time she hosted summer borders and did all the cooking herself, shunning fancy meats or canned goods, and supplying 'homemade country fare'.

biographer says. She served 'newly laid eggs, thick sweet cream, new milk, fresh buttermilk and butter', and the fruits and vegetables were fresh from the garden. Wilder made salad dressing from scratch (home-made cider vinegar, mustard, sugar, egg, salt and pepper) and salads of 'tender lettuce . . . arranged on pretty plates with a hard boiled egg cut in half to show the golden centre and a little ball of cottage cheese'.

Despite the evidence of her family's experience, Wilder continued to believe in the virtues of the small farm and self-sufficiency. The Little House books were a collaboration between Wilder and her daughter, the writer Rose Wilder Lane, and appeared between 1932 and 1943. They were a form of American myth-making – an effort to rewrite Wilder's childhood of tragedy and desperate poverty. But Wilder did it beautifully. *Farmer Boy*, in particular, is full of food, because, as Fraser points out, it was written in 1933 during the Great Depression when everyone was hungry. Its characters eat buckwheat cakes, fried potatoes, sausages, jams, jellies, doughnuts and apple pie – a 'homely cornucopia', Fraser says, which delivered the comfort that Wilder needed more than her readers knew.

W.B. Yeats

1865–1939

He ate a peacock

What's riches to him
That has made a great peacock
With the pride of his eye?

– From 'The Peacock' by W.B. Yeats

The poet William Butler Yeats was the lynchpin organizer of an event on 18 January 1914, at which the young American Imagist poet Ezra Pound was introduced to elder-statesman and English Victorian-era poet (and controversial Irish rights activist) Wilfrid Scawen Blunt at a specially arranged feast at Blunt's house. As was appropriate for a feast involving seven poets, the bill of fare included a highly symbolic centrepiece: a peacock, presented in the raiment of its own feathers.

Yeats was forty-nine at the time of the dinner, and an influential figure on the British literary scene. A Protestant of Anglo-Irish descent, he had become interested in Irish legends, mysticism and the occult at a young age and began writing poetry. In the political context of the time, an interest in Celtic legends and Gaelic heritage was seen as supportive of Irish Nationalism. Yeats became a central figure in the Irish Literary Revival, a founder of Dublin's Abbey Theatre, and twice a Senator for the Irish Free State.

The young Ezra Pound befriended Yeats in London with an eye towards harnessing the older poet's social and literary position in order to create a new kind of poetic establishment, according to Lucy McDiarmid, author of *Poets & the Peacock Dinner.* McDiarmid's book describes several dinners involving an overlapping cast of poets as showing 'a professional group coalescing around a dinner table' and being germinal to the spirit of the age. Apparently, promoting poetry required glamour and high living: at one such dinner, McDiarmid reports, the American poet Robert Frost and several English poets dined on a ham, a joint of beef, a raised pie, birds, fruit tarts, trifles and cheesecake. The hosts were 'especially generous with the cider; at the end of the meal the poets were too drunk to stand'.

The peacock dinner, which was written up afterwards in multiple publications, was held at Blunt's West Sussex manor house in an oak-panelled living room, with a beamed ceiling, stone floor and large fireplace. Pound, McDiarmid writes, had originally envisioned the dinner taking place at a restaurant in bohemian Soho, and hoped that attendance by the anti-establishment Blunt would put it on the map as a social happening and literary provocation. However, the elderly Blunt did not like to travel, so Yeats and Abbey Theatre co-founder Lady Augusta Gregory brokered the deal to hold the event at Blunt's house. McDiarmid's original research discovered that it was Lady Gregory who suggested peacock for the menu, inspired by 'The Peacock', a new poem that Yeats had recently sent her. She also wrote to Blunt that the dish would be appropriate because Yeats had long wished to try peacock, and had been disappointed when it was promised at another event and then not served.

As was appropriate for a feast involving seven poets, the bill of fare included a highly symbolic centrepiece: a peacock, presented in the raiment of its own feathers.

Yeats's poem about the peacock celebrates the bird's aesthetic qualities, and values artistic accomplishment over money. Ezra Pound, consciously styling himself as Yeats's progeny, wrote a poem about Yeats writing 'The Peacock'.

'so that I recalled the noise in the chimney
as it were the wind in the chimney
        but was in reality Uncle William
downstairs composing
that had made a great Peeeacock
        in the pride ov his oiye
        had made a great peeeeeeecock in the . . .
made a great peacock
        in the proide ov his oyyee'
– Ezra Pound, Canto LXXXIII

Pound's poem celebrates artistic cross-pollination, and values the act of writing itself. Blunt was a representative of an older tradition. He thought Yeats wrote 'thin stuff' and 'indifferent verse', according to material quoted by McDiarmid, and found Pound's Imagist poetry incomprehensible 'word puzzles' that a child could write. But nonetheless he accepted the younger poets' desire to honour him, and had a bird killed and hung from his personal flock of peacocks (a decorative item for country houses at the time).

To serve this at a feast was not common in Sussex in 1914, but it was a tradition in England in the Middle Ages and goes back to Roman times, when fabulous presentations of exotic items were often valued more than the actual taste. The ancient preparation method involved skinning the peacock with feathers intact and then separately salt-curing the skin and roasting the bird (sometimes with its neck staked vertically for a more dramatic appearance), reuniting the two just before service. At Blunt's house, McDiarmid reports that the plumage was brought in with a flourish first, 'arranged over a dummy to look realistic', followed by the roasted bird. The poets all took several helpings, and some partook of a roast beef main afterwards.

We don't know if Yeats liked the peacock, but Blunt recorded in his diary that it tasted like turkey.

Index

Credits

The publishers thank the following for permission to reproduce the recipes and quotes in this book. Every effort has been made to provide correct attributions. Any inadvertent errors or omissions will be corrected in subsequent editions.

8 'Caramel Cake recipe', 'Caramel Syrup recipe', and 'Caramel Frosting recipe' from *Hallelujah! The Welcome Table: a Lifetime of Memories with Recipes* by Maya Angelou, copyright © 2004 Caged Bird Legacy, LLC. Used by permission of Random House, an imprint and division of Penguin Random House LLC. All rights reserved; **49** from *Home Cooking* by Laurie Colwin, copyright © 1988 Laurie Colwin. Used by permission of Writers House LLC acting as agent for the author.; **91** from *The Hemingway Cookbook* by Craig Boreth, copyright © 1988 Craig Boreth. Used with permission of Chicago Review Press, permission conveyed through Copyright Clearance Center, Inc.; **187** from *The Cantos of Ezra Pound*, copyright © 1948 Ezra Pound. Used by permission of New Directions Publishing Corp. Used by permission of Faber & Faber Ltd.

Acknowledgements

When I first had the idea of trying to make the food from the pages of a novel, I thought it would be fun, but possibly 'too ambitious.' Eight years later, the project has consumed more of my life than I could ever have dreamed – I made not just one dish per book but five, sometimes more, then threw a dinner party, which turned into a home-restaurant dinner series – and now has sprawled to include the writers' lives and their favorite foods in the book you now hold in your hands.

Many people have helped along the way. I would like to thank the talented staff at *The Paris Review* over the years: Lorin Stein and Nadja Spiegelman, who believed in my cooking-from-literature project at its inception; Emily Nemens and Lori Dorr, who nearly turned Eat Your Words into a TV show; Brian Ransom, who did much of the editing, followed by Sophie Haigney; and Emily Stokes, who continued to believe in the column in its third era; plus well-wishers at the board level, Sandy Gotham Meehan and Jeffrey Eugenides. Photographer Erica MacLean has been my companion on marathon cooking days, a frequent recipe-tester when the pictures are done and brings more life and movement to a plate of food than seems possible.

Many writers and artists who featured in the stories either were or became friends: musician Tetsuro Hoshii, novelist Celia Dovell Bell, painter Heidi Howard and the podcast kids, Kassia Oset and Dylan Cuellar, hosts of Unburied Books. People who have provided meaningful insight into the authors for *The Writer's Table* or during my years cooking from literature are: director of the Jane Austen House Museum Sophie Reynolds, Steve Abbot's daughter Alysia Abbot, Laurie Colwin's adult child RF Jurjevics and Colwin friend Willard Spiegelman, Amparo Dávila translators Audrey Harris and Matthew Gleeson, Sergey Dovlatov's daughter Katherine Dovlatov, John Ehle friend Terry Roberts, Goethe scholar W. Daniel Wilson, writer and Hilda Hilst translator John Keene, writer Joyce Johnson for her words on Jack Kerouac and academic Audrey Sprenger for her advice on Kerouac, D.H. Lawrence biographer John Worthen, program director at the Thomas Mann House in Los Angeles Benno Herz, Herman Melville biographer Andrew Delbanco and writer Caleb Crain for his work on Melville, Iris Murdoch scholars Miles Leeson and Francis White, Flannery O'Connor biographer Brad Gooch and Cassandra Munnell at Andalusia Farm.

I would also like to thank my editors at Compact magazine for helping me move from cooking-from-literature to reviewing it, Sohrab Ahmari, Matthew Schmidtz and Geoff Shullenberger; and editor Matthew Kirby, who has acquired my cooking-from-books skills for a new monthly column for *Our Sunday Visitor Magazine*. Illustrator Katie Tomlinson has made *The Writer's Table* look beautiful, transforming my maximalist urges into something serene and elegant. Victoria Granoff and Victoria Flex provided creative inspiration and food-historian advice. Veronika Sheer loaned me pots and pans and pitched in on wine tasting. Father Kevin Chalifoux has promised to put this book on his coffee table. The wonderful editorial team, Anna Watson and Izzy Toner, have been consistently cheerful, helpful and patient. Friends and dinner guests are too numerous to name, as are all the many people who have reached out online over the years (hi, Michelle Smart, Tao Leigh Goffe, and Fr Jack Bentz, SJ) but a few people who have provided moral support for thirty-plus years: Melissa Checker, Deirdre Dolan, Jeff Howe, Alden Jones.

Lastly I would like to thank my family: my father Sam Stivers, my brother Elliot Stivers, and my two children Adeline Isakov and Tima Isakov (for never eating the weird food, and somehow always needing lunch just in the middle of a photo shoot, thanks guys). Most especially I thank my mother Marilyn Stivers, whose creativity, motivation, taste, perfectionism and desire for things to be fun, have made me what I am, and who has provided unbounded material support, from sourcing table stylings to fighting the squirrels for acorns (so I could make acorn flour for acorn scones from Mary Shelley's Frankenstein, naturally). No project is 'too ambitious' for her, and thus here we are.

Quarto

First published in 2025 by Frances Lincoln,
an imprint of The Quarto Group.
One Triptych Place, London, SE1 9SH, United Kingdom
T (0)20 7700 9000
www.Quarto.com

EEA Representation, WTS Tax d.o.o., Žanova ulica 3, 4000 Kranj, Slovenia
www.wts-tax.si

A catalogue record for this book is available from the British Library.

ISBN 978-0-71129-391-5 • Ebook ISBN 978-1-80570-214-6

10 9 8 7 6 5 4 3 2 1

Design by Nicki Davis

Publisher Philip Cooper
Senior Editor Michael Brunström
Project Manager Anna Watson
Editor Izzy Toner
Senior Designer Isabel Eeles
Senior Production Manager Alex Merrett

Printed in Guangdong, China TT062025